THE DON'T SWEAT GUIDE
TO RETIREMENT

Other books by the editors of Don't Sweat Press

The Don't Sweat Affirmations
The Don't Sweat Guide for Couples
The Don't Sweat Guide for Graduates
The Don't Sweat Guide for Grandparents
The Don't Sweat Guide for Parents
The Don't Sweat Guide for Moms
The Don't Sweat Guide for Weddings
The Don't Sweat Guide to Golf
The Don't Sweat Stories
The Don't Sweat Guide to Travel
The Don't Sweat Guide to Weight Loss
The Don't Sweat Guide to Taxes
The Don't Sweat Guide for Dads
The Don't Sweat Guide for Teachers
The Don't Sweat Guide for Newlyweds

THE DON'T SWEAT GUIDE
TO RETIREMENT

Enjoying Your New
Lifestyle to the Fullest

By the Editors of Don't Sweat Press
Foreword by Richard Carlson, Ph.D.

New York

This book is not intended to offer specific legal, tax,
accounting, or financial advice. Readers should consult with
their financial consultants, as the tax code can change each year.

Hyperion books are available for special promotions and premiums.
For details contact Hyperion Special Markets, 77 West 66th Street,
11th floor, New York, New York 10023, or call 212-456-0133.

ISBN: 0-7868-9055-X

FIRST EDITION

10 9 8 7 6 5 4 3 2 1

Contents

Foreword

In my book *Don't Sweat the Small Stuff at Work,* I mentioned three clubs that people sometimes choose to join. First is the TGIF club. This means "Thank God it's Friday." These members seemingly live for the weekends. They love Fridays, but loathe Mondays. The second club is for the real workaholics. It's called TGIM, or "Thank God it's Monday." Members of this club hate the weekends because they can't get to work! But the club I encourage everyone to join is TGIT, or "Thank God it's Today."

The idea is somewhat self-explanatory. You learn to appreciate and flourish within your current set of circumstances. This works wonders as you enter the world of retirement because, along with the perks, there will be some inevitable but unexpected sources of stress, as well. The idea is to be able to keep those more stressful moments in perspective, to take them as they arise and gently let them go.

In my opinion, retirement can and will be a glorious time in your life. You'll love the freedom and ability to try new things. It's a new phase of life; a chance to be a beginner again. I believe these positive traits will be most enjoyed by having the least amount of expectations about what it's going to be like. Be open to each new experience with a beginner's mind.

Instead of trying to figure it out, see if you can take it one day at a time. Each day, try to appreciate how different your life has become instead of trying to compare it to earlier days. The happiest people I've met in retirement are those doing just that—taking it one step and one day at a time, comparing it as little as possible to days gone by.

The editors of Don't Sweat Press have done a marvelous job at identifying many of the possible sources of stress having to do with retirement, and then cleverly finding ways to keep that stress under control and within one's perspective. When I read the book, it reminded me that most of what I choose to get upset about is largely due to my own thinking. I realized that I have more power within my thinking and my attitude than I sometimes realize.

I think the editors of Don't Sweat Press have provided a terrific companion for the newly retired person. There is plenty of great, fun advice that can put you on the best possible path. I hope you enjoy the presentation as much as I did and that you are flooded with new sources of inspiration like I was.

I congratulate you for picking up this book, and send you good luck in your new life!

Richard Carlson
Benicia, California, 2003

THE DON'T SWEAT GUIDE
TO RETIREMENT

1.

Your World—and Welcome to It!

Retirement is an experience unlike any other. If you're a long-time retiree, you know that this period of life brings unprecedented opportunities and challenges. If you've just ended your career or are contemplating retirement, you're about to embark on a journey at once exciting and demanding, a voyage rich with discovery if you chart the right course.

Retirement doesn't bear much resemblance to your career years. During that chaotic period, you struggled to keep up with demanding schedules that might have been imposed on you by others. Nor is retirement very much like childhood. You had few responsibilities then, but you were too young to be equipped for long-term goals.

Retirement is a unique experience. It is a time when you set your own goals; which of them you pursue and achieve is mostly up to you. You dream as you did in childhood, but now you have the experience and skills to make those dreams come true.

To be sure, a successful retirement depends to a certain extent on finances. Those who haven't saved sufficiently for retirement may find their possibilities limited. If you haven't begun saving for your retirement, don't delay any longer. You'll be surprised how much you can accumulate with even a modest savings program.

Beyond money, though, retirement is more about attitude than anything else. There was a time in our history when retirement was a dirty word, a brief and empty time of life that led to nowhere special and wasn't worth the wait. Those days are over, and a new attitude has led people to celebrate the perks of retirement. Today's retirees are energetic and proud. They're joiners and they're networkers. They're seekers and they're discoverers. They gladly accept responsibility for their own fulfillment, and then they go out and pursue that fulfillment in ways that previous generations could only imagine.

That's the thrill and the challenge awaiting you. Retirement is your world now—welcome aboard!

2.

Your AARP Card

When you look back on where you've been, your most vivid memories may be associated with special occasions, those milestones that seemed to define the periods of your life. The first day of school. Graduation. Wedding day. The births of your children. Each of these events signaled the end of one phase of life and the beginning of a new stage that would introduce more challenges and opportunities.

The age of fifty brings another such milestone—the receipt in the mail of your membership card to AARP (formerly called the American Association of Retired Persons), the national organization dedicated to the interests and needs of retirees. Everyone receives one when turning fifty. Even though you get the card, whether or not you join AARP is entirely up to you.

For some, opening the mail on that fateful day is depressing; they mope around for days thereafter. No matter how youthful they look or feel, it's now official—they've grown older. It isn't that they weren't aware of the passage of time, but to them, the AARP card serves as formal confirmation of a new, undesirable status.

This can be a damaging way to view the milestone of your fiftieth birthday and your retirement—or impending retirement, if you're still at work. In retirement, you'll have the option to explore roads not taken and dreams that may have been shelved for years. There's a good chance that you'll enjoy excellent health while doing so. You'll be able to pursue your favorite activities and undertake new adventures as well. You'll spend as much time as you want with family and friends, and you'll have the opportunity to cultivate rewarding new relationships.

Moreover, as a retiree, you won't have to worry about being marginalized, society's afterthought. Retirees today are a large, organized, powerful group; when they speak, everybody listens.

Retirement *is* a new chapter in your life, a chapter filled with wonderful discoveries, characters, and possibilities. When you get your AARP card, consider it your passport to this world of wonder.

3.

The Changing Face of Retirement

If you've just ended your career or soon will, you're doing so at a time of dramatic and historical change in retirement that promises to bring greater opportunities for fulfillment. For one thing, retirement lasts longer than it used to. When our great-grandparents ended their careers, they could anticipate no more than a brief retirement; they worked straight through to age sixty-five and couldn't reasonably expect many years beyond that. Today, people are not only living longer, but they're experiencing good health later into their lives.

According to the U.S. Census Bureau, women who celebrated their sixty-fifth birthdays in the year 2000 could look forward to an additional 19.2 years, on average; men who turned sixty-five that same year might expect another 16.3 years, on average. When you combine longer, healthier lives with careers that can end well before the age of sixty-five, you have the formula for a long, satisfying retirement.

You also have the opportunity to enjoy a retirement that's better financed than those of your forebears, who typically could count on Social Security benefits and not much more in their later years. Even Social Security is a relatively recent innovation. Consider how people in the nineteenth century must have struggled without it. The advent of such savings vehicles as individual retirement accounts (IRAs) and 401(k) plans has enabled many people to develop the resources for an exciting retirement rich with travel, education, hobbies, and community service.

Contemporary retirees are now recognized as a powerful and important force. In the past, it was possible to shunt retirees to the edges of political consciousness because their numbers were so few and retirement was so brief. That won't work today. National organizations such as AARP and its more than 35 million members promote the interests and welfare of people fifty and over. As a group, retirees are highly valued by product manufacturers and advertisers, who know buying power when they see it.

Today's retirees are active, respected, and sought after—and there are more of them than ever before. Now is the most agreeable environment ever for retirement—and it will only get better.

4.

Who Are Today's Retirees?

In the year 2000, the U.S. population included 35 million people age sixty-five or older (76 million age fifty or older), meaning that about one in every eight Americans is a senior citizen. While that's an impressive number, it only suggests what will happen over the next several decades as the Baby Boom generation marches *en masse* to retirement.

According to the U.S. Census Bureau, by the year 2030, the sixty-five and older age group will soar to 70 million and represent a full twenty percent of the American population. No one can say exactly how many people in the sixty-five and older group are officially retired—the census bureau figures include retirees, part-time workers, those who are looking for work, those who can't find work, and those who never worked. And of course, the sixty-five-and-older figures would not include those under sixty-five who have retired, an ever-expanding group.

What we do know is that retirees come from all walks of life. Retirees today are people who've worked at physically demanding jobs, who now seek nothing more than rest and relaxation. They're fifty-five-year-olds who hunger for retirement adventures. They're former military personnel and civil servants whose lucrative pensions allowed them to retire early and launch second careers.

Retirees have diverse interests—electronic communications among them. Census bureau figures show that in the year 2000, nearly one-quarter of the 21.8 million homes where the householder was sixty-five or older had a computer; nearly eighteen percent of sixty-five-and-older households enjoyed Internet access. While the percentages are substantially less than the figures for the general population, that gap is likely to decrease as more people with computer and Internet familiarity leave the workforce.

That's going to happen sooner rather than later. In a 2001 survey by the Employee Benefit Research Institute, forty-four percent of respondents indicated that they plan to retire before the age of sixty-five. If that remains true, it's sure to give the modern image of retirement a more youthful, vigorous character.

5.

Why Retire at All?

People are living longer and staying healthier longer, so they can be productive members of the workforce well past what many consider the normal retirement age. In addition, many companies have eliminated mandatory retirement rules, facilitating continuing employment. In light of these circumstances, why should anyone retire?

Indeed, for some people, retirement will not be the most attractive option. These folks want most of all to continue on the job, to be part of the company team, because that's what gives them the most satisfaction. Even as the number of retirees has grown, the number of people working through their sixties and seventies has increased, as well.

According to the U.S. Department of Labor, in the year 2000, 12.8 percent of Americans sixty-five and older were part of the civilian labor force, an increase of about one percent from 1990. The percentage is projected to continue climbing through the year 2010, at least.

What we're seeing, perhaps for the first time in America, is the development of options for people of retirement age. For most of our history, careers that extended beyond the age of sixty-five were the exception. You were expected to retire then, and retirement wasn't anything to look forward to—a relatively brief period marked by declining health and limited opportunities due to limited funds.

But the aging of the Baby Boom generation has produced significant changes in the conventional wisdom. As a society, we've created a number of new savings vehicles, such as IRAs and 401(k) plans, to help people finance retirement. We have health insurance programs that assist people in staying fit and active. We've seen the formation of national organizations to advance their interests. And we've tweaked our work rules to enable people to stay on the job longer, if that's their desire.

It all adds up to choices—many more than were available to our parents or grandparents. Think of it as the Golden Age of Retirement, when you can elect to stop working or to keep working, and know that you'll find solid support either way.

6.

Scotching the "Youth Will Be Served" Theory

We're moved to retire by many factors, some more persuasive than others. Perhaps the best reason for retirement is the desire to move toward self-fulfillment. A goal-directed retirement is very likely to be exactly the rewarding period that you envision.

Stepping aside only to make way for someone else is a much less compelling reason for retirement, yet people hear it all the time: *If my retirement allows them to hire a younger person with a growing family to support, I'm doing the right thing.*

Noble as it seems on the surface, this approach may be less than ideal. First, you're not doing your employer any favors. At this point in your career, you're much more valuable to your employer than any neophyte could be. You have a broad variety of skills and vast experience with the company. You *know* things. Your employer can tap that knowledge, which would be hard to acquire on the market. A new hire, on the other hand, will have a lengthy learning curve.

Your company will need to invest significantly in training for your replacement—an investment that will be lost if the young gun doesn't stay with the company.

Moreover, in purely personal terms, young people have options. They're able to relocate more easily than you, and they have many years to acquire and polish skills for the job market. If they don't get your job, they'll have other opportunities—certainly more chances than an older worker with strong ties to a particular community or region.

This is not to suggest that you should adopt a selfish attitude regarding young job-seekers. You can coach and support them. You can mentor them while you're still on the job, in effect training your replacement, and you can remain available for advice after you've retired. That's a winning approach for all concerned.

There's no need to step aside before you're ready. You're as entitled to personal and career satisfaction as people thirty years your junior are. Youth *will* be served—but there's no requirement that you be the waiter.

7.

When to Say "When"

If you've said it once, you've said it a thousand times: "I can't wait until I retire." It's a common response to frustration on the job. You're given a directive that you know will be overturned a few days later. You're caught in an endless, unproductive meeting that's keeping you from your real work. You emerge from an annual review session with a smaller increase than you anticipated. It's then that retirement starts to look good to you, and you catch yourself uttering the infamous phrase.

Retirement can be a golden period chock full of adventure and fulfillment, but only if you approach it for the right reasons and in the right frame of mind. Temporary setbacks on the job may not be the right impetus for a happy retirement. In those cases, it could be that a new assignment, a new boss, or even a new job could restore the satisfaction of your career.

Knowing when to say "when" is vital. Retiring at the right moment will help ensure that you're ready for this new phase of your life and not in need of a less dramatic change, such as a vacation. As you ponder retirement, here are a few key questions to consider.

- Do you long for pursuits, such as travel, exercise, hobbies, and public service, that your work schedule prevents you from undertaking?

- Do you want to become a more diversified person with broader experience and a deeper understanding of the world around you?

- Are you excited by the prospect of filling sixteen hours each day with activities of your own choosing?

If you answer yes to these questions, you may indeed be an excellent candidate for retirement, with all of its opportunities and challenges. Remember that retirement is more than a flight from work. It's a step toward self-actualization. Retirement is progress "to," not a retreat "from." If that's the way that you envision retirement, it may be time to say "when."

8.

Become Who You
Always Wanted to Be

When you were young, your dreams were large. You would wow the sports world with last-second heroics to win the championship for the home team. You would reign in the laboratory, where your pioneering work would cure the world's most feared diseases. You would write the Great American Novel, give bravura musical and stage performances, or persuade soldiers to lay down arms.

Somehow, your dreams of personal glory and saving the world were deferred or abandoned. As you matured, you replaced your dreams with more workaday concerns, such as landing a job and raising a family. While these may have seemed like garden-variety achievements next to your childhood fantasies, they were anything but that. If you fashioned a successful career and nurtured a family, your accomplishments are quite significant. You're an achiever— and that's all the more reason to dream anew.

Retirement is the time to become the person that you always wanted to be. With your reduced load of daily responsibilities, you have the opportunity to pursue all of the goals that you used to dream about. Thanks to the experience and expertise that you've developed over the years, you have a much better idea of how to accomplish your objectives.

Some retirees are reluctant to pursue their childhood dreams, fearing that they no longer have the physical or intellectual capabilities that those pursuits demand. You've heard it said, for example, that childhood is the best time to learn a musical instrument, because youngsters' brains are at an optimal developmental stage for learning. Yet as an accomplished adult, you have the patience and interest that will keep you practicing, perhaps long after many children would become bored and give up.

Where retirement is concerned, the conventional wisdom sometimes isn't very wise. Don't let anyone set your limits for you. In fact, don't post any limits at all until experience suggests that modification is in order. Childhood is a time for dreaming; retirement is a time for making dreams come true.

9.

Your Retirement Checklist

Retirement is an adventure that will lead you to new skills, insights, and satisfactions. If you regard retirement as negative—that is, as nothing more than the absence of work in your life—you're not considering this journey in all of its glorious possibilities. Look at it this way. The typical career lasts about thirty years. With good health, your retirement may endure as long as your career did.

Such a lengthy and important period in your life demands more than a haphazard approach. You don't want to fall into retirement; you want to jump into it with a well-considered game plan. In fact, it's a good idea to develop a checklist that covers the major preconditions for a successful retirement. Make sure that these items appear prominently on your checklist.

Health insurance. If you've been relying on employer-provided insurance, your coverage could end the day that you walk out the door. What type of private coverage will be best for you now, and how can you coordinate it so that your new plan begins as your employer's coverage ends? This is an item for rapid action.

Budget. Many retirees lose their principal source of income once they stop working. If that's the case with you, will you have sufficient money from other sources to cover your expenses? That's where a budget comes in. You'll have a handle on both income and expenses; you'll know when you can splurge and when you must cut back. You may have operated without a spending plan for most of your life, but unless you're independently wealthy, retirement demands budgeting.

Domicile. You're not tied to your job any more, so you can live anywhere you choose. Are you happy in your current home? Do you need a smaller house that's less expensive to maintain? Would an apartment work better for you? Would you be healthier living in another climate? All are good questions, but unlike the issue of health insurance, domicile issues typically don't require immediate solutions. You can take your time to come up with the most agreeable arrangements.

Communication. Ongoing contact with your work friends will be vital in maintaining your sense of connectedness. Make sure you swap home phone numbers and e-mail addresses with your colleagues. Spread your contact information around liberally, and collect as many phone numbers and addresses as you can.

10.

What Happens If
You Can't Cut It?

People expect retirement to be the golden era of their lives, when they enhance their relationships with family and friends, take on exciting new challenges, and finally accomplish their most cherished goals. Indeed, for many people, retirement will be the crowning achievement of their lives.

For others, though, retirement just won't work out. Money will be the culprit, in some cases. With financial experts advising that a successful retirement can require anywhere from $500,000 to $1 million, depending on individual needs and lifestyles, early retirement won't be an option for some. Even if you calculate that you have enough money to finance a comfortable retirement, extraordinary circumstances can wreck your plans.

Some also may find that retirement doesn't suit them. Only when they leave work do they come to fully appreciate how much their careers meant to them. They miss the satisfaction of contributing to a team effort, the repartee with their work friends—they even miss the peculiarly rewarding sensation of ripping open a pay envelope every two weeks. No matter what retirement activities they try, they can't generate the same fulfilling feelings that work brought them. They become restless, itchy, irritable—not the attributes of a happy retirement.

If this sounds like you, don't fight it. If full-time work is what you find most rewarding, then stay on the job—or get back on the job, if you've already retired. Don't think of yourself as a failure. For you, retirement has been a journey to self-awareness. It's given you a firmer sense of who you are and what you want. You've gained much in your brief retirement—and you'll be better prepared when you finally hang it up for good.

11.

On Double Dipping

The trend toward early retirement has brought with it a new phenomenon—double dipping. This occurs when people in certain fields—such as the military, firefighting, police work, teaching, and other public-sector jobs—retire with full pensions after as little as twenty years on the job. Because they're still young and vigorous, many of them begin second careers, receiving a salary and benefits even as they collect their publicly funded pensions. They're dipping into two income pots simultaneously, so that's where the term "double dipping" comes from.

Double dipping has been around for awhile, but it's become more prevalent as benefit packages in some job categories have improved. As you might expect, lucrative pensions provide a powerful incentive for early retirement.

If you encounter double dippers, you may feel a surge of resentment every time that they chat about their great deals. It's taxpayers such as you who are funding these rich pensions and underwriting double dipping, and what benefits are you getting from this? While your feelings may be natural, the envy you feel probably isn't justified.

It's wise to remember that many double dippers worked in the most dangerous or thankless fields of public service, providing defense from our country's enemies, or protecting our homes and communities from criminals and the ravages of fire. Some may have suffered injuries or permanent disabilities. If they're making out a little at the end of their public service careers, is that such a terrible price to pay for the valuable services that they rendered?

Besides, you can be a double dipper, too, by creating your own pension plan to finance your early retirement. If you save through such vehicles as 401(k) plans and IRAs, you may be able to retire early enough to begin a second career while you enjoy distributions from your retirement accounts.

You won't be a double dipper in the classic sense—it's *you* who'll be funding your pension rather than taxpayers—but you'll still reap the financial rewards and the psychological satisfaction of multiple income streams. With proper planning, double dipping is something everyone can enjoy.

12.

Winding Down at the Office

O nce you announce your retirement, your last days on the job may take on a dreamlike quality. You can't really get involved in long-term projects, since you won't be around to see them through. You're not invited to committee meetings, since the work of those committees will continue long after you've retired. Even the quality of your e-mail changes—dozens of congratulatory messages, nothing of any real substance.

With few concrete tasks to perform, it's easy to feel extraneous or to yield to feelings of nostalgia, kicking around the good old days with any of your colleagues who have the time to reminisce with you. Go ahead. There's no harm in a brief trip down Memory Lane. But then put these last few days of employment to good use.

Check in with the personnel or human resources office to make sure that your final payment includes everything to which you're entitled, including conversion of any unused vacation days to cash. If you're participating in any post-retirement plans through your employer, such as health insurance, make sure all of those documents are in order. If you're transferring assets that the company held for you—a 401(k) plan would be an example—finalize and double-check the transfer documents.

You may be interested in an ongoing relationship with your company for project work or mentoring. Now is a good time to let your supervisor—and other key executives—know your desires. You may even be able to line up projects now, jump-starting your retirement with some consulting income.

Use this time to reinforce your relationships with your work friends. You may be surprised and embarrassed to discover that you're not sure of home phone numbers and addresses for many of them. Record those now, along with e-mail addresses, and make sure that they have your contact information. The exchange will help you socialize with your friends when you're no longer a part of their work scene. Make plans to get together with them and to participate in company events—golf outings, picnics, the annual college basketball pool—where you'll surely be welcome. Effectively using your twilight time at the office will help ensure the dawning of a sunny retirement.

13.

Throw Yourself a Retirement Bash

In the classic version of retirement, men and women toil in the vineyards until they reach the age of sixty-five, when company policy forces them to retire. They're feted at a celebration, toasted by senior management, and given a token of the company's appreciation—the symbolic gold watch.

This stereotypical retirement scenario has been squeezed at both ends. Today, many workers are retiring much earlier than sixty-five, determined to pursue their own dreams as soon as possible. For those others whose primary satisfaction comes from work, companies have liberalized their retirement policies or abolished them altogether. For the most part, people can continue to work as long as they're interested and able.

The retirement dinner and gold watch belong to a different era. Rare is the contemporary company willing to allocate precious resources to retirement celebrations when there are so many more pressing needs.

If your employer is unable or unwilling to recognize your impending departure, throw your own retirement bash. Invite those colleagues that you most care about to your gala. It can be something as quick as cupcakes in the lunchroom or as formal as dinner at your favorite restaurant. (As you invite your friends, remind them not to do something crazy and expensive, like pitch in for that gold watch. You want their company, not their gifts.)

Your party will have symbolic value, representing the divide between your career and your retirement, and it can serve several more tangible purposes. For one, the people who shared your world for so many years will be there with you. It will be an opportunity to express your feelings for them, and for your friends to do the same for you.

In addition, you can use your retirement bash to lay the groundwork for post-retirement socializing. Let your friends know what you'll be doing, how they can reach you, and how you can get together in the future. Extending your relationships with your colleagues will take some effort since you'll no longer be seeing them as a matter of course. Begin that effort at your very own celebration.

14.

They'll Struggle
Along Without You

When you're contemplating retirement, don't be surprised if you find yourself pulled in different directions. Retirement—the chance to spend more time with your family and become the person that you always wanted to be—sounds inviting. But you're also driven by a sense of loyalty to your company and your colleagues. What will happen to them if you leave? Will all of the projects in which you're a key player ever be completed? Who will take over the hundreds of work responsibilities that you've assumed, and how will they ever learn to do them right?

If you're tormented by the potential problems at work that your retirement could create, it's a credit to your concern with, and affection for, your fellow workers. Without diminishing the importance of this loyalty, could it be that your concerns are misplaced? Many companies have been in business for decades. They've endured wave after wave of worker retirement. Somehow, the tasks performed by retirees are picked up, and the businesses go on. That same continuity will prevail when you retire.

All of us are unique human beings, yet when it comes to our jobs, all of us are replaceable. That doesn't make our contributions any less valuable. We're inimitable; so are those who follow us. We shine as individuals, yet we're also part of an orderly, immutable succession process. Once you realize this, you'll be prepared to choose retirement without guilt.

There are ways that you can assure a smooth transition without imperiling your well-deserved retirement. Several weeks before you're set to go, begin documenting all of the tasks that you perform, along with a schedule for their execution and a list of the colleagues that you "touch" on each task. This will be far more comprehensive and current than any job description in helping your successor understand the ins and outs of your position.

Also, let your employer know that you're available for consultation should your successor encounter any difficulties. That gives you the best of both worlds—a leg up on retirement, and a hand in the ongoing operations of your former employer.

15.

Your First Few Days

As with all major life changes, retirement requires a period of adjustment before you get the hang of it. The differences between your old and new lives may be most evident in your first few days off the job.

You may find yourself, for example, waking up at your old, career-driven time, only to shake out the cobwebs and realize that you can arise whenever you choose. You may hustle downstairs for that hurried cup of coffee, and then remember that you no longer need to gulp down your breakfast. You can eat at your leisure. Even more disconcerting may be the realization that you have no job or boss requiring anything of you. How you spend your days is entirely up to you.

If you find this an awkward period, there are several ways to ease the transition. First, don't force yourself to new habits prematurely. If you're accustomed to getting up at five-thirty each day, you'll tend to do that no matter what. Don't press the issue.

Get up when you usually do, and don't worry about it. Even if you can't break this habit, it's a small thing. Think of it as a positive. Getting up early gives your day a sharp start.

As for the emptiness that you may feel without work-related tasks, this is easily remedied by giving yourself assignments each day. You don't have to load yourself up—this is retirement, after all. Just give yourself enough to do so that you continue to feel productive and useful during those first few retirement days. Gradually, as retirement begins to feel right to you, you can fine-tune your habits and activity schedule.

Above all, remember that this is a time of change. Think about all of the adjustments that you made when you married, had kids, bought a new home, or changed jobs. Every major life change requires adjustment; retirement is no different. You've always made the proper adjustments before, so you can be confident about adapting to retirement. In short order, you'll have your retirement habits down pat.

16.

The Challenge of
Doing Nothing

Through most of our history, retirement was synonymous with idleness. This approach to retirement made a lot of sense to people of previous generations. Their work was often physical and grueling and the pay meager, allowing little opportunity for retirement savings. So when their careers were over, they may have had little energy or money for much more than relaxation.

Many features of the traditional scenario have changed. Widespread automation has made work a lot less physically demanding for most people. Advances in health care are keeping people fitter and active through their retirement years. The development of pension plans as an enhancement to Social Security has given them the wherewithal to undertake a broad variety of retirement activities. These people are rarin' to go, yet the antiquated notion of retirement as laziness persists.

Doing nothing all day long is perhaps the greatest challenge—and the greatest danger—faced in retirement. It's difficult to be idle for lengthy periods without feeling antsy—even isolated or abandoned in more serious cases. People are social creatures who need to contribute to human endeavor throughout their lives. That's one of the ways that we validate our own worth.

Yes, you can lounge around all day if you choose, and you can sleep in as late as you want, but chances are that this approach to retirement will get stale pretty quickly. A better plan might be to think of retirement as an opportunity to create your own daily schedule, focusing on those activities that bring you the most satisfaction.

When you ask retirees why they're doing what they're doing at a given moment, all too often the response is: "I'm just killing time." Your time is too precious to kill. Enrich time. Ennoble it. Enjoy it. It may be a challenge to use your time effectively, but that's insignificant compared to the challenge of doing nothing.

17.

Try the Thoroughbred Approach

The transition from the world of work to a life of leisure may be more difficult and dangerous than it appears. Think of it. For about forty years, your days have been barely controlled chaos, filled with demanding tasks at work and equally important jobs on the home front. It was a challenge to get everything done, but you managed it. Just as significant as your actual accomplishments was the self-image inspired by your multifaceted achievements. At some level, you came to regard yourself as a dynamo who took on more responsibilities than were humanly possible—and darn near achieved them all.

So what happens when you step over the great divide into retirement? Unless you do something proactive about it, your to-do list becomes alarmingly short—gone are all of the career-related tasks. It's no problem now accomplishing everything on your list; you can do that before noon. The peril here is that with much less required of you, you won't regard yourself as the same competent person that you've always been. Your self-image could take a major hit.

One way to assure a smooth transition is to employ the approach that trainers of Thoroughbred horses long have favored. Being the high-spirited and habitual creatures that they are, Thoroughbreds fret about any change in their routine; stop their training in anticipation of retirement and they sometimes worry themselves into illness or injury.

To prevent that, many trainers take a "step-down" approach to the retirement of their steeds. On the first day, they may take the horses out for their usual rigorous exercise. Days or weeks later, the horses gallop only briefly rather than working against a clock. The next step is to have the horse walk quietly before being turned out to pasture. It's a gradual transition over a few weeks so that the changes aren't too dramatic too soon. The horses have a chance to adjust while still thinking of themselves as champions.

You can adapt this tapering method to your own situation. Instead of going cold turkey into retirement, you might try to work out a part-time arrangement with your employer that will help ease your transition. Schedule tasks for yourself; no matter how arbitrary these might seem, they'll enable you to achieve goals and continue to regard yourself as the champion that you are.

18.

If You Get Withdrawal Pangs . . .

As you settle into retirement, you may find yourself uncharacteristically restless and uneasy. These feelings may be most keen when you're at loose ends—no particular tasks to do, no one with whom to enjoy them anyway. In these awkward moments early in your retirement, you may be tempted to scour the employment ads and apply for the first job that seems even halfway appropriate, so long as it will give you a well-defined schedule and a regular group of colleagues.

No matter how powerful this temptation may be, it's a good idea to resist it, at least for now. Retirement represents a major shift in your life—perhaps the most dramatic change that you'll ever undertake. You've moved from a set schedule with a built-in network of friends to days filled only with the activities and relationships that you cultivate. It's natural to go through an adjustment period and to experience occasional withdrawal pangs.

Think back to the other seminal events that helped transform your life. When you wed, your days changed irrevocably—only to change once again with the births of your children. When you relocated to a new community, when you began a new job, you experienced the same period of anxiety before you formed new habits and new friendships that helped restore your comfort and confidence.

Retirement can be unsettling. Rare is the person who marches into retirement without periodic longings for the life that used to be. Give yourself time. You'll overcome your sense of displacement, just as you adjusted to life's other major changes, but it won't happen overnight.

When you get those withdrawal pangs, ask yourself what's triggering them—what was it about work that you found especially rewarding, and how can you fashion retirement activities that will bring you the same satisfaction? If you continue to find retirement unfulfilling after giving it a fair chance, then it may be appropriate to consider taking on part-time or full-time work. During those early days of retirement, however, it's better to analyze your withdrawal pangs than to succumb to them.

19.

You're a Valuable Resource

The Baby Boom generation—those folks now about ready to swell the ranks of retirees—has been incredibly productive. It's the generation that led us through the development of computers, full speed ahead to the Information Age, and onward to the growth of artificial intelligence. They were the leaders of the civil rights and environmental movements. In communications, they brought us cable television, cell phones, and VCRs. In social services, we can thank them for HMOs and PCPs, if "thank" is the operative word. It's clear that this generation has exerted a profound impact on our daily lives.

What happens when you take all of this expertise out of the economy? Nothing less than a "brain drain" may result, with too much know-how going to the sideline at once. Of course, not all Boomers will retire simultaneously, but the great exodus of these folks from the labor force soon will begin. This is more than a hypothetical concern. For family-owned and closely held businesses, to cite one example, the insurance industry estimates that sixty-five percent won't survive the transition to the next generation. Those firms will miss the expertise and experience of the founders.

With so many of our business leaders poised to retire, the adverse effects on our society can be far-reaching. You can help reduce the impact by remembering that you're a valuable resource.

Think of how your company operated when you first started working there; compare that to how it functions today. The changes probably have been comprehensive—and you're a walking, talking newsreel of those changes. You may be retiring, but you still can make your vast expertise accessible to the new generation. Let your employer know that you're available to help coach or mentor current executives. If you've preserved documents, make those available, as well. If your records are substantial, you might even consider donating them to a local library or university for study by scholars.

You also can formalize your ongoing involvement through such organizations as the Service Corps of Retired Executives (SCORE), which provides volunteer expertise for a broad variety of companies. You may be retired, but you've still a vital job to do—providing the continuity between generations that will keep them moving forward.

20.

Keep Up Appearances

With the growing popularity of casual attire in the workplace, dressing for work may not have been the burden that it once was. Nevertheless, many people still harbor the fantasy of release—slipping into a pair of cutoffs, going unshaven, trawling for marlin in the Florida Keys. If this is your notion of retirement, then pursue it by all means.

For most people, though, keeping up your physical appearance will continue to be important. The effort that you invest in grooming and attire will get you in the right mood for achievement.

This doesn't mean that you can't cultivate a more relaxed look or cut down on clothing purchases. If you can save money in these areas, that will help you stick to your budget. However, in your retirement, you may get less feedback about how important you are. When you dress nicely, you reinforce a strong self-image.

Others will get the message, as well. How wonderful it is that simply by attending to your physical look and taking care with your appearance, you can inspire others, as well as yourself.

21.

You Are *Not* What You Produce

When they sever the ties with their employees, some retirees struggle to define themselves. If they're no longer creating goods or delivering services, who exactly are they? This dilemma has soured retirement for many. It's a good question—questions about identity always are—but many retirees look for the answer in the wrong places.

First and foremost, remember that you are not what you produce. In earlier times, when the vast majority of citizens tilled the soil or handcrafted tools and furniture, this linking of personality and production may have made more sense. People poured their creativity into their jobs; what they produced often was a reflection of their individuality.

The Industrial Revolution helped weaken the bonds between personality and production, reallocating manufacturing among hundreds or thousands of workers at a single plant, with each laborer having only the tiniest responsibility for a finished product.

Recent trends have broadened the personality-product divide. In today's so-called "new economy," it's common for employees to change jobs every two or three years. If they define themselves by what they produce, they'll be forced to reinvent their self-images with every career shift, a dangerous and hopeless mission.

For all the distance that people have come, they still tend to overemphasize the importance of career in personal worth. When they meet someone, they invariably ask, "What do you do?" as if they can truly understand others only by knowing their jobs. While defining yourself by your work makes much less sense than it used to, it's also clear that leaving your company does deprive you of valuable institutional identification and support. Being a key player at a successful company was important, but it was only a part of who you are.

You are not what you produce, or at least not *only* what you produce. You are the sum total of your actions, your insight, your experiences, and your relationships with others. Your personality is multifaceted and ever-evolving; you don't stop growing because you've ended your career. In fact, you have the opportunity to grow in many directions at once because you're no longer required to devote half of each day to work.

Now, when someone asks what you do, you can advise them that you're on a journey of self-discovery that will last the rest of your life. Your products are awareness and fulfillment, items that never lose their value on the market.

22.

Be Proud of Your Status

R etirement doesn't mean that you've ended your contributing role to society. Rather, it's the end of one phase of your participation and the beginning of another, a period in which you have the opportunity to contribute in new and exciting ways. Yet too many people feel diminished in their retirement, worrying that they no longer count as much as those still in the workforce.

Sheer numbers tell a different story. If there are 35 million people age sixty-five and over, and if by the year 2030, one in every five people in the United States will be at least sixty-five years of age, the size of that group should tell you that retirees no longer can be marginalized. This is a powerful group, and you're an important part of it.

If you doubt it, simply turn on the radio or television and pay attention to what's advertised. Home improvement devices, medical products, travel services—all targeted to you. Advertisers are speaking directly to you and your fellow retirees because they respect your needs—to say nothing of your buying power.

While you were working, there's no doubt that you were a valuable member of your professional team and of society in general, yet your contributions may have been confined to the workplace. In your retirement, you have the opportunity to broaden your role by mentoring young people, supporting nonprofit organizations, performing public service, or becoming active in politics—all contributions to society for which you may have had little time during your career. You can become more intimately involved with your community than ever before—a role that should fill you with pride.

Chances are that you've motored up behind a car and noticed that it was bearing a bumper sticker that said something like "Retired—and Proud of It!" You may have chuckled at the time, but now you appreciate that the contributions of retirees are worth shouting about. If you feel the urge to honk in response or slap a similar strip on your own car, go ahead and do it. That's exactly the confident, proud attitude that you should display in your retirement.

23.

The Fine Art of Mentoring

When you retire, you take with you the knowledge and experience developed over the course of your outstanding career. What a shame it would be if all of your expertise were lost to the next generation because of your retirement. You can prevent that from happening by serving as a mentor for aspiring young workers.

Mentors play a key—though often unacknowledged—role in most successful careers. There's much for young people to learn about their specific companies and industries, and about the world of business and life in general. Mentors can help guide them to the right choices and avoid mistakes that could be career-threatening.

For all of its value, mentoring is a more delicate art than it seems. Most people need to feel in charge of their own lives and choices, even if those choices bring disastrous consequences. Sometimes, we need to fail on our own, even if a mentor could have helped us avoid failure. Thus, your style as a mentor should be subtle. Let it be known that you're available to help, even if only as a sounding board for ideas. Touch base with your charges, but let them introduce problems or challenges that may be troubling them. An odd thing about advice: The more delicately it's offered, the more willingly it's taken.

You can mentor family and friends, but your most eager candidates will probably be the staff at the company where you worked; your expertise will have the most value there. In fact, your old employer might be willing to formalize a mentoring relationship with you so that you become a consultant on a paid basis.

Consider the case of Jack Roseman, who founded several companies and served on the faculty at Carnegie Mellon University before retiring in 2000. So many young entrepreneurs continued to approach Jack for his advice that he formed an entity, the Roseman Institute, as a base for his mentoring efforts. Today, well into his supposed retirement, for a fee, he helps early-stage technology companies identify top executive talent, funding sources, business partners, and customers.

That kind of fee is rare, but financial reward isn't your primary goal here. You will earn the satisfaction that comes with nurturing a fellow being. Mentoring also will serve as an affirmation, reminding you that what you know is well worth knowing.

24.

A Great New Relationship

As you edge toward retirement, you may find it tempting to back off a bit on the job; to forget your usual conscientiousness in favor of a more blasé approach. After all, you'll be gone in a matter of days or weeks. If you're not as fastidious as you've always been, what difference will it make? It can't damage your annual review or chances for promotion—you'll be long gone before those would come up.

Yet doing less than your best in the face of impending retirement *can* be damaging. Perhaps most importantly, it can impair your image of yourself as a caring, competent person with a commitment to professionalism. You may not haul off a king's ransom in retirement savings when you punch out for the last time, but you *can* emerge with your full complement of self-respect. That means doing your best until the very last moment of your employment.

There are practical reasons, as well, for remaining on excellent terms with your employer. You may be eligible for employer-sponsored benefits or a pension program for retirees. If you maintain a good relationship with your company, they'll be happy to resolve any problems with your benefits and respond promptly to your inquiries.

Staying close with your employer can also lead to other advantages. A favorable letter of recommendation should you need a reference for any part-time work or new career; consulting projects that may become available; the opportunity to participate in company social events and mentor young staff—all of these benefits could be yours if you remain in good standing with your company.

As your workdays dwindle down to a precious few, don't think of yourself as a short-timer. Instead, view yourself as an elder statesman whose wisdom and experience are valuable assets that your former colleagues can tap. If you bestow this emeritus status on yourself, you may find that others come to perceive you in exactly the same way.

25.

What's Up with Social Security?

You've no doubt heard this story in one or more of its frightening variations: "The Social Security system is going broke." If you've fretted about it, you're not alone. Despite the growth of private savings vehicles, forty percent of American workers cite Social Security benefits as their principal source of retirement income, according to a 2001 survey by the Employee Benefit Research Institute.

In 2002, the trustees of the Social Security Administration issued a report to clarify the status of the program. They indicated that the trust fund has sufficient funds to pay full benefits until the year 2041 and seventy-three percent of expected benefits thereafter. It was a good news/bad news document. The good news is that there's no threat to your benefits for the immediate future. The bad news is that the long-range solvency of the program still must be addressed.

President George W. Bush took a stab at it by creating a commission to study the future of Social Security. In 2002, when the commission offered three recommendations that all involved some degree of privatization—allowing covered workers to invest part of their Social Security taxes in private markets—it evoked a firestorm of controversy.

AARP criticized the recommendations for what it called lack of balance. "People will have to work longer, pay more and risk getting less," AARP executive director Bill Novelli predicted. Dr. John C. Goodman, president of the National Center for Policy Analysis, speculated that without some degree of privatization, "the tax rates future taxpayers will have to pay to keep the system going are astronomical." The Cato Institute joined the fray by introducing its own plan that included a wrinkle—privatization backed by a government-funded safety net to assure minimum retirement benefits for all. The National Committee to Preserve Social Security and Medicare also weighed in with its oft-stated position—to protect the current system "from those who would privatize it and leave today's and tomorrow's retirees with risky individual investment accounts that rise and fall at the whims of Wall Street...."

The debate showed pretty clearly that consensus about the future of Social Security has yet to emerge. The discussions will continue. Follow them, and let your congresspeople and senators know how you feel. This is policy in the making that can be influenced by those with the most to gain or lose.

26.

Forming New Social Networks

Many people like to think of retirement as placid, a time of reduced responsibilities when they can take life as it comes. If that's the retirement that you envision, create it and enjoy it. Yet there's one area of retirement that may require a bit more work—ensuring that you have sufficient social contact to keep your sense of worth as high as it's always been.

A diminished level of human contact—beyond the superficial level—is one of the ever-present dangers of retirement. You never had to worry about this while you were working and raising your family. At work, you had an instant network of friends, ranging from buddies to confidants. At home, child-rearing activities put you in touch with many other adults in the same situation. Whether you were attending the class play or participating in a PTA meeting, you met other parents and made new friends.

Now that these natural socializing opportunities are gone, it will be important for you to replace them with new relationships and networks. Go beyond occasional chats with the postal carrier and clerks at the supermarket—though such give-and-take can be part of the equation. You want your new relationships to be deeply rewarding and long-lasting.

Factor socializing opportunities into all of your retirement activities. If travel is a key part of your retirement itinerary, think about group excursions that can bring you close to others. When you're developing hobbies, consider those that will allow you to share your discoveries with fellow hobbyists. If public service is a retirement goal of yours, pick a civic activity that improves your neighborhood—and lets you work regularly with others.

Relationships will reinforce your self-image as a valuable, contributing member of society. Don't wait for them to happen. Take the initiative. Socialize in as many venues as you can. You'll soon form so many fruitful relationships that you'll never face the pain of disconnection.

27.

Strike a Balance
with Your Family

Retirement gives you the opportunity to be with your family. In fact, the desire to strengthen familial relationships can be the driving force in your retirement. It may be part of what motivated you to stop working, and it may be where you now want to spend most of your time.

Achieving those stronger family bonds, however, may require more effort than you think. You regard your kids and their kids as integral parts of your family, of course, but remember, they constitute a nuclear family of their own—several families, if you have more than one child. Your family really may be an extended group of families, each with its own needs and styles. It's important to balance your needs and theirs. You can achieve that balance in several ways.

Most importantly, discuss your hopes and intentions with your kids, and listen carefully as they share their thoughts on familial relationships. Reach some agreement on when you'll visit them, when they'll come to see you, where you can help them financially, and where they prefer to do it themselves. These can be difficult discussions. You may not be used to structured conversations within your family, but if everybody's needs are expressed openly, that will prevent friction later on.

Pay special attention to holiday protocol—nothing can sink the ship of family harmony faster than ill will around major holidays. Perhaps you've always hosted family gatherings for the holidays. Now, though, your children may want to take over that role; it may represent something of a rite of passage for them. Instead of feeling hurt, try to work out a compromise. Alternate holidays, say, or help your children with the cooking and other preparations at their homes.

Don't hesitate to express your preferences. If you have an opportunity for a bargain cruise that will take you away for the holidays, let your kids know what you're thinking. Their flexibility may surprise you. If you're being overused as a baby-sitter, speak up. Let your children know when you're available and when you'll be pursuing other retirement goals. They'll almost certainly work out a new schedule with you. More than anyone, your kids have your best interests at heart.

28.
Ah, the Grandkids!

Many people have a tendency as grandparents to spoil their grandchildren—and that can ruin the time spent with the young ones and wreak havoc with their parents, as well. Here are a couple of thoughts on staying close with your grandkids.

Follow any behavioral or nutritional rules that your children have established for their children. Make sure that you enforce bedtime. If your children give their kids healthy snacks, don't sneak in sugar-filled treats.

If your grandchildren are in those awkward teenage years, they may need to establish their space. Let them pick the conversational topics, at least for openers. Once they relax, they'll be more receptive to your questions.

Technology is a great place to start. If you allow your grandchildren to advise you on the operation of your new computer, for example, that will give them an opportunity to achieve something by helping you. In addition to the warm feelings that you'll get when your grandchild confides in you, you'll pick up some sound technology advice!

29.

Achieving Remains Important

Retirement may be a time for shedding some responsibilities, but it doesn't signal an end to achieving. Establishing goals, accomplishing some, modifying others to reflect new circumstances and needs—all of that should remain a key part of your retirement game plan.

Your goals will change, sometimes dramatically. No longer will you need to worry about work-related problems, for example. That in itself should bring welcome relief. But don't view that as the end of goal-setting. Think instead of substituting new objectives that may be more relevant to this period of your life.

Retirement goals can involve family and friends. If your work schedule prevented you from maintaining ties with those closest to you, plan to touch base with them more regularly. Spending time with them will bring pleasure into your life and theirs, and help you achieve one of your key objectives.

Your goals should include developing a full and varied roster of activities. This is a mission that can occupy you throughout your retirement. If you do it successfully, you'll earn double-barrel rewards—the specific pleasure that your participation brings, and the bonus satisfaction that comes with goal achievement.

If you've been a "list maker" all of your life, unable to proceed with any day until you have it documented and organized on paper, don't stop just because you've retired. The items on your list may change; your organized approach to achievement need not.

Don't confuse retirement with drift. Achieving, and the planning that goes into it, remain important in every phase of your life. When you commit to achievement, what you're really saying is that you're looking forward to the future, and that you fully expect to be a vital player in that future. Then when you realize your goals, you affirm and strengthen your self-confidence. Keep achieving, keep affirming. Your accomplishments in fresh, new areas will provide the psychological and spiritual foundation for your success in retirement.

30.

The Joys of Travel

O ne of the most gratifying aspects of the new-look retirement— a
period in which many of us are blessed with unprecedented
physical and financial resources—is the opportunity that it provides
for travel. When you're no longer tied to a job, you have the chance
to explore lands that you could only dream about before.

Travel can become perhaps your most rewarding retirement
activity. The whole world is beckoning. Every pristine beach, every
jagged peak, every lush forest, and every bustling metropolis is yours
for the taking. You can visit spots that long have sparked your
imagination—and explore others that are completely unfamiliar to
you. Either way, travel is a unique experience that provides
entertainment and enlightenment at the same time.

When you travel, you get a firsthand view of how others live,
what they eat, how they think about things, and how they perceive
you and your country. You get to know people in ways that books,
travelogues, and the Internet can only suggest. Your hosts, of

course, discover the same things about you, leading to new levels of multicultural understanding. This may be one of the great, unheralded virtues of travel. You learn that you have much in common with people throughout the world, leading to bonds that tend to discourage hostilities.

This is as true of travel within this country as it is of excursions abroad. America is a melting pot, a country of many cultures shaped by differences in history, geography, and other factors. Hitting the road can acquaint you with your country's people, in all of their dazzling variety. Whether you choose to stay close to home or explore distant locales, travel is broadening—for you and for the people that you encounter.

Travel satisfies a very human longing—to learn about others and to have them discover you. Now is the perfect time for you to satisfy that longing.

31.

Become a Techno-Maven

Retirement isn't about clinging to the old ways. It's about exploring, discovering, growing. To the extent that technology can help you achieve your goals, embrace it.

Welcoming technology to your retirement doesn't mean that you must have every new gadget that comes on the market. However, a portable phone could ensure that your family can reach you wherever you are around the house. Voice mail could guarantee that you never miss an important message. A compact disc player will let you enjoy the music that you like. A camcorder will help you preserve the precious moments of your retirement. A personal computer will help you explore options for your future.

These are the technologies—once cutting-edge, now everyday—that can enhance your retirement, and it won't take you long to master them. Study them. Adopt them as your needs and budget dictate. You'll become a techno-maven, and your retirement will be more satisfying for it.

32.

The Hobbyist

Most people remember childhood as a particularly fertile period for hobbies. Before they were introduced to career and family responsibilities, they collected stamps, coins, matchbooks, or model airplanes, and they experienced a flush of excitement each time that they added to their collections or spent blissful Saturday mornings reorganizing them.

If you've led a busy life, chances are that you haven't dusted off your old collections in years. Retirement is a great time to return to the hobbies of your youth—or to launch new endeavors.

Hobbies can involve just about any activity that you pursue in a repetitive or comprehensive way, and you can structure hobbies to your needs and preferences. Reading, for example, can be a rewarding hobby; if you regard that as too passive, you can satisfy your interest in literature by collecting signed first editions of your favorite books. Regular exercise is a healthy hobby—but if you find an exercise regimen too taxing, supporting your favorite teams can get you involved in sports in a less demanding way. Once you determine an area of interest, it's easy to find an approach that works for you.

One thing to keep in mind as you revisit or create hobbies—these pursuits often carry a price tag. Daily workouts may require purchase of exercise equipment or membership in a fitness center. Becoming a diehard sports fan may involve the purchase of game tickets, as well as travel and parking costs at sporting arenas. If your hobby involves renovating cars or other types of equipment, you may have to lay out money for parts. In some cases, however, hobbies can lead to moneymaking ventures.

Remember to add a line in your retirement budget for hobby costs. Your hobbies don't have to generate revenue for you—creative engagement is the principal purpose here—but if they do, so much the better.

33.

Financing Your Retirement

Your financial health is a vital factor in a long and successful retirement. When people retire, they typically leave behind their principal sources of income. Yet their fundamental needs don't change. Developing revenue sources to make up for the loss of their wages becomes a priority.

Estimates of the financial requirements for a retired couple range from $500,000 to $1 million in assets, depending on the desired lifestyle. During the stock market boom of the late twentieth century, many people thought that they had this challenge licked as they watched the value of their holdings soar. Unfortunately, that was followed by an extended market slump that cost people millions in their worth—on paper, at least—and pushed back retirement for many.

How serious is the problem? A 2002 survey by the Employee Benefit Research Institute and the American Savings Education Council indicated that less than twenty-five percent of workers between the ages of forty and fifty-nine have saved more than $100,000. A coalition of consumer and credit union groups later that year issued a report showing that a quarter of U.S. households have assets of less than $10,000.

These figures may be worrisome, but they shouldn't discourage you. Instead, learn from them. Develop a plan now that will produce sufficient income for the happy—and early—retirement you may be envisioning.

Saving will be the cornerstone of your blueprint. Take the fullest advantage of any savings plan, such as a 401(k) account, that your employer may provide. When you max out your contribution, your employer is obligated to do the same. If you're not offered such a plan at work, consider your own savings vehicle, such as an IRA.

Save as much as you can, even if it means small sacrifices now. Cutting several days from your vacation for the next several years, for example, will enable you to reallocate the money you save to your retirement's financial package. If you've already retired, continue to save. The one thing that can be predicted about the future is that circumstances will change. If you keep building your assets, you'll be a master of change rather than its victim.

34.

Cast Yourself Against Type

In your retirement, you have the opportunity to create any role for yourself that you choose. Go a little crazy and cast yourself against type. Of course, this isn't to suggest that you abandon those retirement dreams that you've been nurturing for years. Those always should remain your priority. But think outside the box. Take on a challenge that you've always dreaded or feared.

Have you avoided dancing all of these years because it made you feel awkward and conspicuous? Take a dance class. How about cars? If you hate dealing with automobiles because you're intimidated by their complexity, it's high time to get under the hood and dive in.

Casting yourself against type, and developing new skills, can bring you more satisfaction than you ever imagined possible. Not only are you rounding out your personality and developing new skills, you're tackling challenges, a sure sign of personal growth.

35.

When to Do It Yourself . . . or Not

Your retirement gives you plenty of hours to allocate as you see fit. You'll want to devote much of your time to pursuing your top retirement goals, of course, but you also may want to dedicate part of your schedule to household maintenance and repairs. Generally, this is a terrific idea. It improves your home—for living and sale purposes—and you save money on all of those contractors that you used to engage.

It's important to apply a little common sense to any new do-it-yourself approach. Everyone has their limits. If you've shoveled snow from your walk and driveway all of your life, you may be reluctant to engage one of the neighborhood kids who knock on your door with an offer to shovel. Yet snow shoveling can become a dangerous activity as people age. If you are ill or out of shape, hiring a youngster will be a few dollars well spent—on preserving your health.

Many chores—cleaning the gutters is a good example—present increasing perils for us as retirees. Where tasks require a high degree of coordination and strength, we may be better advised to bring in some help.

Still other household responsibilities demand sophisticated expertise in complicated disciplines. Troubleshooting your computer is one such area; fiddling with electrical wiring is another. Even though you have the time now to work on these nagging problems, their complexity and potential dangers suggest that hiring outside experts is a better way to go.

When the task demands it, don't hesitate to get help. This may be a concession to age, but it's not an indication of failure. Think of yourself as the manager of home repairs and improvements rather than the laborer. Bring all of your career skills to bear—select your contracting candidates, compare rates, check references, demand estimates and contracts, and monitor progress. If you effectively manage these tasks, you *will* be doing it yourself—in the broadest and most important sense.

36.

Preparing for Your Trips Abroad

By now, you probably have your vacation drill reduced to a neat science. You know which suitcases you want, where to stash your clothes and toiletries, where to get traveler's checks at the best price, and when to arrive at the airport. Yet if international travel is on your itinerary, you'll have a more extensive preparation list. Here are some points to cover before converting the world to your oyster.

Touch base with the U.S. State Department. No, the secretary may not have personal advice for you, but you can check out the official travel warnings on the department's web site (travel.state.gov/travel_warnings.html). In addition to discovering where travel may be unsafe, you can view the department's consular information sheets—summaries of entry requirements, money-changing protocol, and unusual circumstances for each country.

Let folks know where you'll be, and when. When traveling abroad, it's a great idea to provide the local U.S. embassy with a copy of your schedule, particularly if you're visiting lands where communications systems are unreliable. If you encounter trouble, knowledge of your planned whereabouts can help friendly officials speed to your aid. As for phoning friends and family back home, don't rely on random calls. If your calls keep missing them, you may worry needlessly about them, and they may worry about you. Establishing a schedule—"I'll phone you every evening at nine"—might be one approach. Don't forget to account for differences in time zones.

Take care of the little guys. Veteran travelers know how to provide for their pets. If you're just getting the hang of travel, you have a number of options for pet care, including boarding your pets at a kennel or hiring a pet sitter to tend to your pals. Some pet sitters will feed and exercise your animals, while others will board them. Some even will stay at your home to provide round-the-clock care. Fees most often are by the day. If you don't have a pet sitter yet, you may be able to identify one online at the web site of the National Association of Pet Sitters (www.petsitters.org), or the home page for Professional Pet Sitters (www.petsit.com).

37.

How Responsible
Do You Want to Be?

If your retirement isn't always as gratifying as you had hoped, the problem may lie in the area of responsibility—or lack thereof. The traditional image of retirees at poolside, living lives of leisure and accountable to no one, is seductive. Yet it may be based on a false premise—that retirement means lack of responsibility.

Think of what that really would mean. If you have no responsibilities, you're not an integral part of any group or team. Without responsibilities, you're achieving very little, since responsible behavior is at the very heart of achievement. You have no team to back you up and no accomplishments to support your self-esteem. That doesn't sound like the ideal retirement environment for many.

As a society, it may be time to banish once and for all the obsolete notion of retirement as idleness. Instead, the focus should be on balancing responsibility and personal freedom. While people are working and raising families, the scale tilts heavily toward responsibility. In retirement, they can restore the balance and have the best of both worlds.

How responsible do you want to be? It's a good question to ask yourself as you begin your retirement, and a good question to repeat periodically as you evaluate and modify your retirement. If you explore the balance in your life between responsibility and freedom, you'll be better able to decide how much time to commit to others and how much to reserve for yourself.

Every so often, adjustments may be in order. If you find yourself overcommitted, with little time remaining for the pursuits that you treasure most, you can reduce your responsibilities. For example, you might tell your kids that you need some relief from baby-sitting their kids, or you might advise the supervisor of the civic project on which you're assisting that you need a break. On the other hand, if time is weighing heavily for you and you're feeling disconnected from meaningful contact, taking on more responsibility might be just the right treatment.

Retirement is dynamic. Your level of responsibility is a retirement feature that you can change as needed. Keep evaluating and adjusting your commitments to find the most agreeable balance for you.

38.

Some Keys to Social Security

Even as people work toward assuring the long-term health of the Social Security system, covered retirees will continue to receive all benefits to which they're entitled for the foreseeable future. Thus, it's important to understand how Social Security works, or at least to understand its key features as they affect you. Here's a quick look at some of the most important aspects of the system.

You already have your benefits statement. Several years ago, the Social Security Administration began mailing benefits statements to all of those eligible for coverage—meaning everyone who's paying Social Security taxes. The statements, which are updated and mailed annually, reflect the Social Security taxes that you've paid and the benefits to which you're entitled upon retirement. The statement is a useful tool in planning your retirement budget—and another good reason to pay attention to your mail. If you don't have your latest statement, it's easy to get one. You can order a statement online at the SSA web site (www.ssa.gov) or call the agency's toll-free number, (800) 772-1213, to request a statement. Should you need to order one, it's formally called the Social Security Statement.

The age for full retirement benefits is changing. Historically, you could take partial benefits beginning at age sixty-two and receive your full benefits package when you turned sixty-five. The age at which partial benefits kick in hasn't changed, but full retirement eligibility is rising, on a graduated basis, to age sixty-seven. Your eligibility depends on the year of your birth. If you check the table on the SSA web site, you'll find the exact age at which your full benefits can begin.

You can apply for benefits online. You still may schedule an in-person appointment at your nearest SSA office to apply for benefits, but doing it electronically can be more convenient. The SSA has a page where you can apply for benefits (www.ssa.gov/applyforbenefits/). This will get you directly to the application procedures and forms, although you can access them with a couple clicks from the SSA home page if you prefer.

Remember that all aspects of Social Security policies and practices are subject to change. A neat feature of the SSA web site is that you can keep up with any of those changes. If you click on the appropriate button in the Frequently Asked Questions (FAQ) section, the SSA will automatically notify you online of any changes in the areas in which you indicate an interest.

39.

Give Yourself a Retirement Stress Test

When people reach a certain age, it's not uncommon for their doctors to prescribe "stress tests" for them. They're put through the paces on a treadmill or similar apparatus to see how their hearts and lungs respond to the physical challenge. Stress tests sometimes can detect damage that may not have been apparent in their daily tasks and help point them in the direction of treatment.

Retirement can have its own set of stresses, so it may be useful to employ a similar diagnostic tool to determine how you're responding to those pressures. Don't test yourself too early in your retirement—that's still a transitional period that can produce anxiety. Wait until you've settled into your retirement, and then ask yourself this series of questions.

- Do I look forward to each day?
- Am I accomplishing the retirement goals that I established for myself?

- Do I take the initiative in planning activities with friends?
- Am I broadening my understanding, capabilities, and experience?

If you answer yes to each question, you've passed your stress test with flying colors and probably have a satisfying retirement ahead of you. If you have one or more negative answers, it may be time to tweak your approach.

Some sources of stress are more remediable than others. For example, if you've allowed yourself to fall out of touch with friends, it's relatively easy to be more proactive and visit the people closest to you. If you're not accomplishing your retirement goals, it could be that you need a new set of objectives—or even a first set of targets, if you've entered retirement without a game plan.

If you make progress in these two key areas, chances are that you'll reduce stress across the board. When you have more commerce with friends, you'll begin to look forward to each day. When you achieve your goals, you'll broaden your understanding, capabilities, and experience.

Don't wait too long to administer your exam. The sooner you address stress, the happier your retirement will be.

40.

What Happens If One
of You Still Works?

Through all of the years that both of you worked, you settled into some comfortable domestic patterns—perhaps without even planning or discussing them. You and your spouse knew who would be awake first and who, therefore, would bring in the paper, prepare the kids for school, and feed the pets. You knew who would be home first and better positioned to get dinner started. You divided the household chores according to time available and personal preferences. Maybe the formula wasn't always rational, and maybe it was a little messy at times, but it worked for you.

If both of you retire at the same time, your domestic model should still serve you well. What happens, though, if one of you retires while the other decides to continue working? Now, that snug domestic formula that took years to develop can be threatened. Several key elements have changed.

First and most obviously, one partner suddenly has a lot more time available for household chores. It's natural for the working spouse to expect the retired partner to pick up more of the domestic duties. Yet it may be just as natural for the retiree in the marriage to resent the intrusion of domestic details into what is supposed to be the halcyon period of retirement. Clearly, reassignment of chores is an area that requires collective attention rather than assuming that rules of the past still apply.

Perhaps more importantly, if you're the working spouse, you may feel unduly burdened. You, after all, continue to provide the lion's share of the income, and continue to be the source of health insurance through employer coverage, so why shouldn't your retired partner—who has little of consequence to do all day long—take on additional chores and help you out more?

If you find yourself thinking this way, you've fallen into the "you are what you produce" trap. Everyone is equally valuable—retirees and workers alike. That applies to society as a whole, and it applies to your household, as well. Remember that each of you has made a choice. One of you continues to work because that's the best choice. The other has retired because that's the best choice. Each of you is playing a valuable role in your marriage, roles that will continue to be rewarding if they're reinforced by mutual support.

41.

Get a Handle on
Your Income Sources

When your grandparents worked until they were sixty-five, they didn't have to think very long or hard about financing retirement. Life expectancies were in the seventies, so they knew that all else being equal, their retirement probably wouldn't last very long, and they wouldn't need much money for their remaining years.

Things have changed dramatically. Not only are people retiring earlier, but they're living longer. If you and your spouse both retire when you're fifty and maintain your health, you each might have up to forty years of retirement. The financial requirements could be significant, indeed.

Faced with that financial burden, some people postpone retirement until they can accumulate enough money to pay for it. However, don't take that step until you complete a thorough review of your income sources. Include everything that might provide you with revenue—on a regular or a one-time basis.

Think first about wages. If you expect to work part-time in your retirement, you can project that income for your tally. Consider also Social Security payments and all other retirement vehicles from which you might begin taking withdrawals. These would include any and all IRAs, 401(k) plans, and annuities. Life insurance policies also should be in the mix; if your premiums have been buying a "whole-life" policy, you may have been building equity that you now can convert to cash.

Do you have bank accounts that yield interest, or stocks that provide you with dividends? Factor these in, as well. When you consider all of these sources, you'll have a pretty fair idea of how much revenue you'll generate each year. That will get your budgeting process off to a promising start.

One action that you should *not* take immediately is liquidation of your assets to provide a big infusion of cash. Divesting your stocks, for example, will bring you instant inflow, but it's preferable to maintain your assets as income-producing vehicles, if you can. Ultimately, liquidating some of your assets may be a step that you'll want to consider, but you'll first want to develop comprehensive understanding of your income and needs before launching a major sell-off.

42.

Set Your Sights on These Sites

When you become a "Netizen," you'll become enchanted with the Internet and the World Wide Web. There's so much information and entertainment available that you'll find yourself surfing for hours. Here are some great web sites to get your Internet journey off to a good start.

AARP (www.aarp.org)—As you might expect, AARP offers one of the most comprehensive retirement-oriented sites. You can visit departments on health, money, lifestyles, volunteerism, Medicare, and Social Security. You can follow the progress of legislation—both federal and state—of vital interest to retirees. You can keep current with AARP events, publications, and special programs, as well.

Social Security Administration (www.ssa.gov)—Visit this site and you can navigate SSA online, performing many functions that formerly required a phone call or a visit. You can stay on top of any changes in benefits and eligibility.

U.S. State Department (travel.state.gov/travel_warnings.html)—If you're considering international travel, this site will advise you which countries are under official travel warnings. You also can view "consular information sheets," guides to currency, health information, and entry regulations for every nation in the world.

The National Council on the Aging (www.ncoa.org and www.benefitscheckup.org)—The first of these addresses will take you to the council's general site, the second to a more specialized site that will help you learn if you're missing out on key benefits in the health, utilities, and supplemental income areas. This is not a passive search; you must fill out an online form with personalized information to take advantage of the site.

Gray Panthers (www.graypanthers.org)—At this site, you can determine the local chapter of the Gray Panthers, an international advocacy organization; read about consumer "Action Alerts"; and learn the inspiring history of the organization.

Traveler's Journal (www.travelersjournal.com)—Click on the "Archives" section, and you'll find two years' worth of Traveler's Journal radio programs—in text and audio formats—chock full of destination profiles and travel tips. This radio series is no longer on the air, but the archives remain accessible.

All of these sites can be valuable resources throughout your retirement—and they'll link you to scores of additional venues that could prove just as useful. Set your sights on these sites as a foundation for your new web world.

43.

Don't Become a Victim

It's hard to pick up a newspaper without reading of the victimization of older citizens. As people age, they run the risk of becoming more inviting and vulnerable targets. However, there's no reason why you have to be victimized. If you follow a certain protocol, not only will you avoid being duped, but you also may be able to turn the tables on would-be thieves. Consider these steps to arm yourself against victimization.

Demand offers in writing. If an offer is legit, a sales representative will have no problem producing a written version of it. Once you have that, you can review it at your leisure—and if it's a big-ticket item, you may want to have your attorney review the offer, as well. You'll also have a record of everything that's been promised to you in case there's a discrepancy down the road. If you can't get it in writing, you don't have an offer that's worth your time.

Treat your home as your castle. As unfriendly as it may seem, don't invite contractors or sales reps in until they've earned your trust. How can they do that? For one thing, they can produce identification, such as a company ID badge with a name and phone number. Don't hesitate to call the number for verification—even while your visitor is waiting outside. This is prudent, not rude.

Take your time to review offers. Sales reps will press you for a decision right at that very moment, perhaps even indicating that the offer no longer will be valid if you don't act quickly. Don't act quickly. Any reputable offer will stand up to your review. Ask for references, and check them.

Contact proper authorities. If you have any questions about the legitimacy of a contractor, vendor, or sales rep, call the appropriate authorities. It's better to bring them in before you've been victimized than after. If it turns out that you helped uncover some sort of crime, you'll have done a tremendous service for yourself and fellow retirees.

44.

Getting the Hang of Computers

You know where you want to go with your computer; getting there can be quite a journey. When you initially turn on that wonderful machine, you may be temporarily puzzled by the array of options, images, and commands, all of them unfamiliar to you. Don't despair. Think of all of the people in your circle who have become computer-literate. Are they any brighter or more capable than you? Of course not. They did it, and so will you—but it *is* reasonable to get some guidance along the way.

Your computer itself will be a valuable source of information. No matter the operating system, make, or model of your unit, it probably will offer "tutorials"—explanations and instructions for each function available. Typically, you can access the tutorials by clicking on the "Help" button. When you purchase your equipment, you'll also receive a user guide that you can consult for both workaday problems and unusual glitches.

Even with the tutorials, you should anticipate getting stuck— that is, encountering a problem for which you just can't find the solution. Your tech team will be helpful here. They experienced the same or similar problems; they'll be able to help you out of your jam pretty quickly.

Finally, consider taking a course in computer operations. You'll have many choices here. If you select a commercial provider that focuses exclusively on computer training, you're more likely to get a hands-on, practical approach. If you opt for a course at a local college, you may get basic computer theory mixed in with the nuts and bolts. Either approach can work for you, so price and accessibility may be the key factors in your decision.

Don't regard enrolling in a course as tantamount to surrender. Few people master computers entirely on their own. Corporations routinely send their employees to computer class, knowing that instruction will get them up to speed quickly and comprehensively. For you, a class will have benefits even beyond these. It will introduce you to new friends and provide you with a tangible achievement; both are vital aspects of a successful retirement.

45.

Take the Futility
out of Utilities

When you were working, you were probably inundated with offers from providers of telephone, cellular, and Internet service. If you live in a state that permits you to choose your natural gas and electricity providers, the stack of mail that you received each month from utility vendors was truly impressive. Like most busy people, you probably pitched the entire pile into the trash without reading so much as a single offer.

That approach might have made some sense when your time was at a premium. Now that you're not on the clock, it might be worth your while to review the offers. Better service and reduced rates could be waiting—if you follow a few useful guidelines.

First, don't be seduced by the "sign-up" bonuses that some providers offer. The prospect of a quick fifty or one hundred dollars for doing nothing more than filling out a form may seem attractive, but long-term benefits are what should drive your utility decisions.

Well after that fifty or one hundred dollars is gone, will you be saving on your monthly rates? Will your service be better than it is today? Those are the key questions to ask.

Also, consider the track record of those pursuing your business. This is especially true with electricity and natural gas; people depend on these to a greater extent than they might ever acknowledge. The last thing that you want is a disruption in these vital utilities. Do your homework. Go online and check out each vendor's web site. If you have questions about their services, ask them. How quickly and fully they respond to your questions now might be a clue to their performance later.

Once you make your vendor selections, it's important to follow up. Preserve the original offers, and check them against your bills to make sure that you're receiving exactly what you've been promised.

One caveat: If it ain't broke, don't fix it. If you're satisfied with your service and the rates that you're paying for that service, there's no compelling reason to abandon your current providers. Where changing vendors would provide negligible savings over the next year or so, stay within your current comfort zone. You'll get significant satisfaction knowing that your careful research has validated your existing situation.

46.

Your Own Tech Team

Technology can improve your retirement in many ways. It can provide you with communications tools to keep you in touch with friends and family. It can make the lives of you and your spouse more secure. And it can offer you a compelling variety of new activities and challenges.

You may equate technology with computers, a mainstay of our age. Yet the technology landscape is more lush than that. Think of CDs, DVDs, and other entertainment formats; smoke detectors and wireless security systems; cell phones, portable phones, and voice mail. All can enrich your life—and you may find many of these products quite affordable.

There's much to learn about these devices, and many options to consider. One of the most useful projects that you can undertake in your retirement is to research the tools of technology. Probe their capabilities and prices. Determine which would be important additions for you and which would be little more than gadgetry, expensive "toys" that you don't need.

You'll develop a solid foundation of knowledge that you can supplement by building your own technology team. Your children and grandchildren will be great team members. At least some of them are probably "into" technology, and are ready and willing to help you navigate the information highway. Include friends with tech experience on your team, and don't forget your former colleagues. They'll be honored to be part of your squad and delighted that you're keeping in touch.

Perhaps the most important member of your tech team will be the person who can help you with repairs. Even the most sophisticated technology tools malfunction; if you've come to depend on them, you won't want to be without them for very long. Your repair consultant can walk you through the fixes or perform them personally—and also give you guidance on the advisability of maintenance contracts for your equipment. You may not find your repair ace in the phone book; many are freelancers who are supplementing their salaries or run their own small personal technology consulting firms. Their fees often are quite reasonable. Word of mouth will be important in helping you locate and engage a reliable troubleshooter.

As for you, you'll function as the chief information officer for your tech team. That's an impressive promotion for someone who may have resisted technology all these years.

47.

Journeying the World on a Budget

While on vacation, people seldom give much thought to the money that they're spending. Vacations are for living it up, forgetting their cares. Who wants to pinch pennies on Fantasy Island?

This devil-may-care attitude may have worked while you were young and at the height of your earning power. Now, sticking to your budget is a key factor in a happy retirement. Recognize this, but don't let it crimp your travel plans. You *can* enjoy travel, and you *can* travel within your budget—if you adopt a savvy approach.

One way to save money is to book your trips abroad early. Many travel agencies will offer you deep discounts if you're willing to book months in advance. At the other end of the time line, you may realize significant savings if you wait until the last minute to finalize your plans. That could give you the opportunity to pick up plane tickets that carriers will offer cheaply, rather than flying with empty seats.

It's odd that locking into a plan early or deferring scheduling until the last minute each can save you money, but that's the way travel marketing has evolved. Here are some other budget-friendly pointers.

Explore senior fare programs. Many carriers offer discounted coupon booklets for seniors. Typically, you must pay for coupons in advance and use them within a year, but they may not require Saturday night stays, as many discounted tickets do. Some coupons also entitle users to bring a companion—even two, if they're children.

Shop around for the best currency exchange venues. The official exchange rate is only your starting point. Automated teller machines, big banks, and exchange offices often provide the best legal rates. You may not make out as well at hotels, restaurants, and exchange kiosks at airports and train stations.

Spend all of your foreign currency while abroad. If you exchange your money again when you come home, you'll encounter another service fee. If you end up scattering leftover foreign currency atop your dresser, you've spent that money, in effect, and gotten nothing for it—except a messy dresser.

48.

Oh, Those Telemarketers!

You have always been a favorite target of telemarketers, but because you were working and away from home, you may not have realized how frequently they called you. Now that they know you've retired—don't ask how they know; they know—they'll jangle your phone with a steady stream of calls.

Some folks deal with telemarketers by refusing to answer the phone, allowing all calls to go to the answering machine or voice mail instead. This sort of screening can accomplish the goal of neutralizing telemarketers.

If you don't like to screen calls, you can develop a protocol to deal with telemarketers, a set procedure that you follow every time. If you handle each call on an ad hoc basis, you may find yourself seduced by offers that you don't really want. Worse, a call at an inopportune time could anger you, and you don't want these anonymous peddlers to disturb what should be a satisfying period in your life.

Pick your approach, and then implement it. Some prefer a preemptive approach, cutting off all callers after they've identified themselves by name and company—they're required to do that, so if they don't identify themselves immediately, insist that they do so. Others allow telemarketers to ramble on for awhile before politely declining the offers and hanging up.

If you do hear a telemarketer out and are interested in the offer, it's a good idea to ask for it in writing. When they tell you "it's a phone offer only," you'll know not to proceed any further. If they follow up with a written offer, you'll have a record of everything that you're supposed to receive, and at what price.

The bottom line on telemarketers is that it's your home, your retirement, and your peace of mind. Stay in charge of the situation. Don't feel guilty about hanging up or cutting off your caller in midsentence. You didn't solicit the call, and there's no reason for you to be any more polite than you choose to be.

49.

What Shall We Read Today?

Tell the truth: When you were working, did you read as much as you wanted to? Did you experience little stabs of guilt each time you started a novel but never got through it because you were just too darned tired to read after working and getting through all of your household chores? There's no reason to feel guilty about subordinating reading; you had many responsibilities that outweighed the importance of recreational activities. Now that you're retired, that's all changed.

You have all of the raw material that you could hope for—anything ever published is out there waiting for you, and you have all of the time that you need for some serious reading. In fact, you may feel a little overwhelmed by literary choices. As with most aspects of your retirement, a little planning will enhance your reading enjoyment.

Prioritize all of the material that you've been meaning to read, and polish these off first. After that, think diversity. Read a popular novel, and then follow it up with some classic literature. Enjoy a nonfiction book, and then perhaps a biography. Don't forget newspapers, magazines, and the Internet. Even as you're exploring new literary worlds, periodicals and "e-zines" will keep you on top of current news developments. (If you're so inclined, you can accomplish much of your reading at the local library and avoid the expense of purchasing books.)

Build wild and unexpected delights into your reading adventures. If you've never sat down with a volume of poetry before, try it now. You might even read the poetry aloud to get the full effect. If the last play that you read was *Romeo and Juliet* in the ninth grade, pick up something by a contemporary playwright. The raw power of modern theater might surprise and please you.

Don't worry if you don't like every work that you encounter. There's no such thing as a "bad read." At the very least, you discover how one writer sees the world and manipulates language. That's always valuable and well worth your time.

Take a few notes on each book that you read as a way of stimulating thought and chronicling your achievements. You can go even further by joining a local book discussion group. You'll find the conversation stimulating, and you'll expand your social network as you rejoin the literary life.

50.

Join the Pet Set

Retirement is a great time to bring pets into your life. You may have avoided pets during your career, knowing that your busy schedule would prevent you from giving them the attention that they deserved. You have the time now, and you'll find that dedicating some of that time to an animal will enrich your life—and provide a warm, secure environment for a creature in need.

There are some things to consider before joining the pet set. If this is your first walk on the wild side, so to speak, you may suffer a case of sticker shock—the little rascals are expensive. Food is an ongoing cost, but even that pales before the price of veterinary care. When your pets are healthy, you may be lulled into a false sense of financial security that could be shattered when you encounter the expense of vet care.

Wonderful advances in veterinary medicine have helped people prolong the lives of their pets, but only at great expense. People are used to insurers picking up the costs for their own health care, but veterinary insurance is not widespread. Before you acquire your pet, explore the local veterinary scene to determine if any practitioners participate in insurance plans. Factor pet costs into your overall spending plan. Few items can bust a budget faster than extraordinary medical care—for you or your pet.

Think also about your travel plans. It would be unfair to your little friends to be left alone for long periods while you travel, yet it would be equally unfair to you if pet care intruded on your retirement dreams. Consider taking your pets with you when you can. If you can't, inspect local kennels before boarding your pets. Will your pets get regular exercise while they're boarded? Does the kennel require evidence of animals' health before accepting them as boarders? These are key questions to ask.

If you're able to plan for them effectively, pets will add immeasurably to your life, and you to theirs. Caring for them gives a purpose to each day—one of the most important yet elusive of retirement goals.

51.

How to Be a BROC

Because of the way our education system is structured, we tend to think of learning as an eighteen-to-twenty-year episode early in our lives, which then are given over to more practical matters. Yet learning can be a lifelong experience, with knowledge and skills gained in both formal and informal venues.

While you never stop learning, your retirement gives you the unique opportunity to return to more structured education. It's a great time to study those disciplines that always intrigued you. If you haven't looked through a college catalogue for awhile, you'll be excited by the variety of courses available. Auto mechanics, aerobics, horticulture, culinary arts, computers—you'll find courses in all of these disciplines, and more. Some will be practical, and others just for fun.

Many courses combine classroom instruction with field experience. A course in architecture, for example, might include trips to signature local buildings. A session on current literature could feature class discussions at the homes of instructors and students. An oenology course might take you to your community's best wine cellars. These are terrific opportunities to expand your social network as you learn.

If there's no local campus within an easy commute, distance learning is an option. The world is available to you online, as well as in person. Most college catalogs will tell you which courses are offered online.

Beyond learning for leisure, consider a degree—particularly if your pursuit of a degree was interrupted years ago. When you return to school, you'll find that your experience and good work habits make course work a lot easier than it seemed when you were young.

Some retirees are shy about returning to the classroom, fearing that they'll be conspicuous among the mostly younger students. You'll find that traditionally aged students will welcome your participation and the counsel that you can offer. Instructors will be delighted to welcome you aboard. They know that your assignments will be thoughtfully produced and punctually submitted, and that you'll probably be the leader of class discussions. In their eyes, you'll be the BROC—Big Retiree on Campus—just by setting foot in their classrooms.

52.

Give Something Back

You've been fortunate to enjoy a successful career, and you're looking forward to an equally rewarding retirement. Many factors were responsible for your good fortune, not the least of which were your own talents and industriousness. But your community also played a role in providing you with the solid foundation and support that you needed. Now, it's time to give something back.

Retirees long have participated in volunteer work, but for many years, they were shunted to a few more or less traditional roles, such as pushing a gift cart in a hospital. Volunteering at a local hospital remains laudable, but the growing numbers and power of retirees present sweeping new opportunities. It won't be difficult at all to match your voluntary activities with your personal interests.

If you enjoy cultural activities, for example, you'll find that the local symphony, opera, and ballet will welcome your volunteer efforts. If animals are your thing, offer to become a dog walker at your local animal shelter. If you prefer working with your neighbors in need, you'll find plenty of opportunities to deliver meals and support services to folks in your community.

You'll probably come up with dozens of good ideas, but if you're stumped, help is available online. When you visit the web sites of VolunteerMatch (www.volunteermatch.org) or Volunteer Solutions (www.volunteersolutions.org), you can click on a list of public service opportunities in your region. If you key in your preferred interests, you'll get a short list of prospective matches.

Volunteer work will bring you considerable satisfaction even while it provides a valuable service to your community. Remembering several aspects of volunteerism can make your efforts particularly rewarding. First, it's wise to work out a mutually agreeable schedule with the organizations that you're helping. You have other goals in retirement. If you expect to be traveling for extended periods, review your availability with the organization. In most cases, you'll find them quite accommodating. However, they will come to count on you, so it's advisable to develop a schedule that works for all parties.

Also remember to be proactive in seeking the right volunteer opportunities. You'll need to take the initiative, because most organizations won't know that you're interested and available unless you tell them. If you can't find the right opportunity, create one. Is there a scenic stream in your neighborhood that's choking on litter? Instead of waiting for the government to address the problem, organize a cleanup effort. You can accomplish a great deal by bringing your experience and leadership skills to volunteerism.

53.

Become a Joiner

For all of the rewards of retirement, it can impose a feeling of isolation on you. You've lost the sense of community that work provides. Job networks can be somewhat artificial, but they were part of your daily community. Your sense of isolation may be even deeper if your active family life toned down when your kids went out on their own.

You can end your exile by becoming a joiner and establishing new social networks to replace those that may have been lost. Even if you weren't the clubby sort while you were working, now is the time to enroll. You can tailor your new networks to your specific interests.

If you enjoy working out, consider joining a public fitness center (assuming this fits within your retirement budget) rather than exercising exclusively at home. You'll find an appealing diversity of people at the club, fun group outings on the activities schedule, and a great venue for forming new relationships. Exercising alongside a new friend is a bonding experience—think of it as a form of social "sweat equity."

Managing finances is a must for everyone in retirement. You can transform money management into a network-building activity by joining an investment club. You commit only as much money as you choose, and you'll meet some interesting new people. If the money that you invest grows, you realize a nice bonus.

Which organizations should you join? That's an individual choice, but make sure that your participation provides you with opportunities for personal contact. Correspondence by Internet is okay, but face-to-face interaction will preserve your feelings of community.

Speaking of community, you can combine your networking efforts with public service. If there's a neighborhood block watch, for example, it's a great time for you to join the patrol. You'll be getting to know your neighbors even as you contribute something concrete to the betterment of society.

54.

Take the Plunge into Politics

You can structure an entry into the political realm in many ways. A simple way to get your feet wet is to devote more attention to the events around you—and to national and world developments, as well. You can become a dedicated follower of the news through newspapers, magazines, television, radio, and the Internet. If you choose, you can go well beyond that by attending lectures and presentations on current events.

Once you improve your awareness, you'll be a well-informed voter—the best kind—and you'll be poised to express your opinions to your elected officials (even if you don't know all of their names yet). Call them, or send them e-mails. They'll appreciate the input, and you may even find that you can help influence *their* positions.

Finally, consider a run for local office. This is not as farfetched as it may seem. Many candidates for local positions—even statewide offices—run unopposed simply because the minority party can't muster up a candidate. With your new awareness and concern, there's no reason why that candidate can't be you.

55.

You Have Clout!

Today, the Gray Panthers is a nationally prominent organization in the vanguard of activism to improve the lives of retirees and senior citizens. The group even has broadened its mission to include what it calls "intergenerational" concerns, such as access to quality education and environmental preservation. It's an organization that's sometimes admired, sometimes feared, but always respected.

Yet that was far from the case in August 1970, when the late Maggie Kuhn met with four of her friends to discuss their common experiences as retirees. It was from that "klatch" that the Gray Panthers emerged, a tribute to the power that retirees can wield when they work together.

Retirees have clout. As they grow in numbers and political sophistication, they have the ear of elected officials suddenly sensitized to retirees' needs. There are pragmatic reasons for this, of course. Politicians know that older citizens are often the most attentive audience, and they're also likely to vote. According to the Federal Election Commission, in the 1998 general elections across

America, 58.2 percent of citizens forty-five and older voted, while only 33.9 percent of citizens under forty-five did so. Retirees who work together have the opportunity to shape the policies that are most important to them.

You can help exercise this nascent power by becoming part of an action network. It might be a well-staffed organization with a multifaceted mandate. Or you could join an ad hoc network formed around a single key issue. Either way, your involvement will help advance the cause.

If you can't find such networks in your community, consider starting one. You can affiliate with a well-established national organization—you'll likely get plenty of support from them—or launch an entirely new group. Don't be daunted by the prospect of beginning your network from scratch. All that you need are a few key ingredients—a sincere belief in what you're doing, familiarity with the issues of the day, and—history tells us—four like-minded friends.

56.

Develop a New
Marital Protocol

On the face of it, retiring while your spouse continues to work should not occasion domestic upheaval, but your retirement introduces a dramatic change to your union. As the retiree, you now have more time available for household chores—and you may well be expected to pick up more of them. Chained to household drudgery may not be the retirement that you envisioned, but working all day and then performing dreary tasks all evening may not be the dream life of your spouse, either.

Few couples formally divvy up their chores; assignments just sort of happen over time. But if you're in a "split" household—one retiree, one worker—a formal discussion about, and allocation of, domestic tasks may help preserve mutual respect and affection in your marriage. Some assignmenets to consider include cleaning, cooking, dishwashing, laundry and dry cleaning, grocery shopping, bill paying, household repairs, pet care (if any), and automobile upkeep.

As you discuss these common tasks—and any that may be unique to your household—put the initials of the current person who does the job on that line. Now, as you reach agreement on modifications, place the initials of the person who will now perform the job on that line. If you see significant differences between the first name and the second, you're well on the way to a productive new marital protocol.

Get as inventive as you like with the assignments. For example, cooking can be a shared task; one partner may be responsible for meals during the week while the other does the cooking on weekends. Don't feel straitjacketed by your revised domestic schedule. If you're new to cleaning, turn it into a challenge, just like you used to do with those tough assignments at work, by exploring such questions as: What resources will I need? How can I complete this job most quickly and efficiently?

Think of your new workload as "creative domesticity." If you stamp household chores with your own originality, they'll provide you with a sense of achievement—and an appreciative spouse.

57.

Here's How One Couple Does It

When Tim reached the age of fifty-five, he knew that it was time for him to retire. He had run an advertising agency for twenty years, and the competitiveness of the industry had taken its toll on him. In addition, his father, institutionalized with Alzheimer's disease, would require more and more of his time. For Tim, retirement was an easy decision.

Not so for Tim's wife. Terri operated an art gallery. She had become an entrepreneur late in her career and was still enjoying the novelty of running her business—to say nothing of its not inconsiderable profits. Retirement was the last thing on her mind.

When Tim sold his business, he created a classic "split" household—one spouse retired, the other still working. Here's how Tim and Terri made the adjustment.

Household chores were not a problem; neither of them did any. Because their resources allowed them to hire outside help for most domestic tasks, the allocation of such chores never became an issue.

Of greater concern was the imbalance of time devoted to making money. Knowing that this could become a source of friction, they worked out an agreeable formula.

Tim would continue to contribute to their financial success by using some of his time to study the stock market and invest—to a mutually agreed-upon limit. He could visit his health club daily to begin aerobics classes and develop a new group of friends. He also would have as much time as he needed for his father's care.

But there was a kicker. Tim would drive Terri to the gallery each day and pick her up after work. Whenever Terri needed a break, Tim would stand in for her. While he had no knowledge of the "artsy-craftsy biz," as he called it, he had plenty of experience in customer relations and actually looked forward to adapting that to his wife's business. Most importantly, Tim would agree to accompany Terri on her occasional buying trips to ensure that the couple continued to enjoy quality time together.

It's been nearly five years since they formulated their new marital protocol, and it's working famously. Tim made a lot of money buying stocks during the technology boom, and sold many of them before the subsequent downturn. He continues to join Terri on buying trips, helping transform each into a working vacation. They're both content with the contributions and roles of each partner. Theirs is a successful split marriage; each would attribute that success to the mature and rational planning that they undertook before Tim's retirement.

58.

Make Cyberspace Your Place!

For all of the popularity of computers, it's estimated that about forty-seven percent of American households don't have them; residents of such households, therefore, cannot access or use the Internet. Further, older adults are much more likely to shun computers than young adults or kids.

Some fear computers because they don't understand the technology behind them. Computers represent something new, complicated, and scary. Their thinking is, *I've done just fine until now without computers, thank you, and I'll continue to do fine without them.* It's time to transcend this glass-half-empty approach.

Understanding computers, and using them to access the Internet, will open up exciting new worlds for you. Perhaps most important will be the addition of electronic mail to your communications tools. You'll find e-mail a quick and reliable way to communicate; if you can type, however slowly, you'll master e-mail in no time. You'll discover that e-mail is a great way to reach out to children or grandchildren who have grown up in the Information Age; they'll be much more talkative and intimate than they usually are in face-to-face conversation. E-mail is the medium that they're used to, so you'll be meeting them on their own turf.

You'll enjoy many other online options. If travel is an important aspect of your retirement, you can visit the web sites of your favorite destinations. You can plan your itinerary, make online hotel and airline reservations, and even buy tickets to special events at your destination. You'll also find that many of your service providers, such as natural gas, electricity, and phone companies, accept online payments. Your bank may offer online services. You can file your federal income taxes, follow the stock market, purchase or sell just about any goods—all of these through your computer.

When you become part of the wired world, you'll experience a keen and lasting sense of satisfaction at having overcome your computer jitters and acquired a set of skills that are so valuable. No doubt about it—it's time to make cyberspace your place!

59.

A Singular Retirement

When couples retire, either separately or simultaneously, they have the support of their marriage to help ease the transition and make retirement a fulfilling experience. The same can't be said of single people who retire. For them, the abrupt severing of their connection to work friends can lead to a sense of isolation. Successful retirement requires progress toward goals; ending your career is not enough.

What do you hope to achieve by retiring? One retiree thought that his pension would be a passport to happy retirement, but ultimately took little satisfaction in cashing the checks. He didn't realize that camaraderie was more important to him than anything that money could buy.

Take some time to fully understand the person that you are—and the person that you would like to become in retirement. Then you can develop a plan—whether it includes travel, public service, education, or other components—that helps you achieve your retirement goals. With a little planning and self-awareness, your single retirement will be a singular retirement.

60.

Is a Second Career for You?

No matter how much they may have yearned for it, no matter how thoroughly they may have planned for it, some people will be disappointed in retirement. For this relative handful of people, nothing in retirement can replace or even approximate the rush of being part of a professional team and producing tangible results.

If you're restless in your retirement and pondering a return to the workforce, give yourself a little time to see if your dissatisfaction lasts. Introduce some new activities to diversify and perk up your retirement schedule. Should your malaise persist, it may be time to consider a second career.

The great thing about going back to work is that at this point in your life, you know yourself better than you ever did. You're well aware of your professional strengths and shortcomings, and you know what types of work would be most satisfying for you. You're also familiar with the entire range of compensation packages, so you know what to expect—and what to demand—in wages and benefits.

You may be able to combine the best of both worlds by working from your home. This will allow you to preserve some elements of retirement as you earn a paycheck. Even if working at home does nothing more than eliminate your daily commute, that aspect can create ten to twenty additional hours each week for those retirement activities that you find most rewarding.

Perhaps the most important point to remember about launching a second career is to keep your family in the loop. If you're married—and especially if your kids are at home—your family probably made a sizable adjustment when you retired. Now, just when they've come to appreciate having you around, you're about to hit them with another major change.

Keep your family posted on your thinking well in advance of any decision. Consider their counsel, and if you do decide to return to work, give them sufficient time to react and adjust. The more considerate you are of their needs, the more supportive they'll be— whatever your choice.

61.

Part-Time Gigs

However diverse your activities in retirement, you may find that nothing you do matches the satisfaction of work—taking on an assignment, stamping it with your own creativity, and seeing your handiwork become a vital component of a team effort. Many people don't fully realize how much this creative process means to them until they're away from it for awhile. When they do finally understand how fulfilling their jobs were, they may be reluctant to acknowledge it, lest the admission spoil their retirement.

Don't let this happen to you. If you miss the rewards of work, fess up—and then do something about it. While a second career is one approach, part-time work is a great way of combining the satisfactions of a job and the pleasures of retirement.

If you go this route, decide how many hours you'd like to devote to work. Part-time gigs have a way of mushrooming and becoming something like full-time work. If you don't want part-time employment to intrude on other retirement activities, be firm in limiting the hours that you make available for work.

Think also about where you would like to work. Traveling to a work site can mean transportation expenses, as well as time lost to commuting. Working from your home might restrict the opportunities available to you, but it will keep you close to your family and maximize your scheduling flexibility. If you want to work on your projects early in the morning or late at night, you can. A computer will facilitate at-home work; you can keep in touch with your clients online, reducing the time that you must spend at the job site.

Now you're ready to consider part-time opportunities. Former employers can be an excellent source of work—particularly if you've maintained cordial relations with them. Word of mouth can provide some leads, as will newspaper ads.

You'll find that most employers will be delighted to consider you for part-time projects. They know that they can count on your diligence, experience, and punctuality; if they're not paying you any benefits, your fee will be significantly less than what they might pay to hire fully loaded, full-time staff.

It's a good deal for them, and the extra income—to say nothing of the job and its satisfactions—will work for you, too. If you're at full retirement age and receiving Social Security benefits, don't worry about exceeding income ceilings and being forced to give back some of your Social Security money. You can earn an unlimited amount without affecting your Social Security payments.

62.

Pricing Your Work

If you were a full-time employee throughout your career, you may never have sold your work on a project basis. Now that you're contemplating part-time gigs, you'll be negotiating agreements with clients. In learning this new set of skills, think about these three elements: your fee, how you would like that fee structured, and the deadline for completion.

The fee that you propose can be influenced by several factors, including the worth of the project to you, its value to employers, and the time and labor involved. The current market for the type of services that you offer also will play a role. Most clients have a pretty fair understanding of the going rates for freelance services. You don't want to be too far above the norm or you may not get the work, but you also don't want to sell yourself too cheaply.

Talk to folks who buy and sell freelance services to get a feel for current rates, and then decide what each project should yield for you. When you present your proposals to clients, remember that most negotiations involve compromises. Establish a bottom line in your mind, and don't allow yourself to be negotiated below that. Knowing when to walk away is an important aspect of successful independent work.

On fee structure, you'll find as many ways to shape fees as there are clients to purchase your services. Some prefer to pay by the project, while others would rather be billed on an hourly basis—if you can estimate the number of hours involved. Any structure should work well for you, provided it gets you to the fee that you have in mind.

Reach an understanding with your clients about the scope of services and the deadlines for completion. Push for deadlines that are as generous as possible. You're taking on part-time gigs for the additional income and gratification that they bring, not to revisit the deadline pressures which you experienced in your career. Remember that you'll need to invoice your clients before they can pay you, and that all of your income from part-time work must be reported for tax purposes.

One final piece of advice: If you're dealing with new clients, it's advisable to insist on up to fifty percent of your fee up front. When you're engaged for a project, you're betting that the client will pay in full, just as the client is taking a risk—that you'll submit acceptable work on time. Getting half of your fee up front is a good way of sharing these risks with your new clients rather than shouldering the entire burden yourself.

63.

Say No to Telemarketers
Once and for All

According to AARP, there are about 140,000 telemarketing firms in America generating $260 billion in annual revenue. If only five percent of those companies are scam artists, that leaves 7,000 potential thieves lurking on the other end of your phone. It's a scary specter—and far from fanciful. Congress estimates that telemarketing fraud costs American consumers more than $40 billion each year, a staggering loss.

Developing a protocol to deal with unsolicited offers will help keep you from being victimized. However, you may want to go even further and say no to telemarketers, once and for all. There are several ways to opt out of telemarketing calls.

The easiest way, AARP suggests, is to verbally advise telemarketers who call that you no longer wish to be disturbed. You must inform each telemarketer of this as you receive their calls. Under federal law, most telemarketers are required to keep and respect "Do Not Call" lists. If they violate your privacy after you've opted out, you may be eligible for financial damages.

If verbal instructions strike you as too tentative, you can put your request in writing—on a postcard or in a letter—to the Direct Marketing Association at this address:

Telephone Preference Service
Direct Marketing Association
P.O. Box 9014
Farmingdale, NY 11735-9014

Include your full name, address, and signature, and expect your request to be activated in about three months. It will be honored by all members of the Direct Marketing Association. The association also includes members that deal in direct mail and e-mail "blasts," so if you'd like to opt out of these unsolicited communications, you can request that of the association in the same manner.

Beyond federal law and voluntary guidelines, more than twenty states maintain their own laws regarding telemarketers and direct mailers; many of the statutes include opt-out provisions, so these are worth researching.

Remember that only reputable firms will adhere to opt-out laws; scam artists will pay little attention to them. Nevertheless, just saying no to telemarketers and direct mailers should significantly reduce your volume of unsolicited communications, and make it easier for you to deal with those who do get through.

64.

Thinking About Transportation

People are able to quantify expenses for most budget items. They know what it costs for such categories as housing, electricity, water and sewage, and Internet access because they get the bills each month. However, if you use an automobile as your principal means of transportation, you'd be hard-pressed to determine how much it costs you each year to maintain your car. You know what car insurance costs because you're invoiced for that, but how much do you spend on repairs and maintenance? How much on tolls? How much on gasoline?

In each case, the probable answer is "a lot." Transportation costs pose a threat to your retirement budget; if you don't know how much you spend, you don't know how much to allocate, or even if you have sufficient funds to cover this category.

Do you still need a car? It's a good time to find out by getting a handle on your transportation costs and alternatives. For a few months, keep a record of your automobile costs. (If your spouse drives a separate vehicle, keep a tab of those costs, as well.) After three months, you can annualize the costs by multiplying the total expenses by four. This won't be an exact figure—some costs are seasonal—but you'll be in the ballpark.

With that figure in hand, explore other transportation options. Review maps and routes of the bus and subway systems in your town to determine if these means of transport would be workable for you. Look also at cab and limousine companies—don't forget any personalized van services that may be available to senior citizens in your town. Calculate what you would save by using public transportation, and then determine if the savings justify the inconvenience.

Public transportation will not be a viable option for some, even if it is far cheaper than maintaining a car. Your local public transport system may not be far-reaching enough to serve you properly. Or you may be counting on your car as your magic carpet for day trips, family visits, and other important outings. But if you go through this exercise, you'll know how much to budget for your automobile, even if you do find that a car remains essential.

For many, surrendering the car will mean only minor tradeoffs—and major savings. Leaving the driving to others can get you where you want to go—physically and financially.

65.

But Where Shall We Go?

In selecting destinations for travel, you're faced with an embarrassment of riches. Each site seems more attractive than the next; choosing one may mean elimination of the others, a potentially stress-inducing process that is not what you want from retirement.

There are a few variables to consider when selecting a travel destination. Foremost in your thinking should be the safety of you, your spouse, and any others in your travel party. Avoid locations where conflict or diseases are prevalent. Check the travel bulletins issued by the U.S. State Department and you'll get a good sense of destinations to avoid—at least until conditions improve.

Next, factor in your personal preferences. If you have a particular interest in wildlife, plan journeys that will get you up close and personal with nature. If you've always been fascinated by New Orleans during Mardi Gras or you've harbored a secret desire to observe the running of the bulls at Pamplona, now is the time to indulge those fantasies. They need be fantasies no longer.

Think, too, of your own health and comfort needs. If you have a low tolerance for heat and humidity, there's no reason to torture yourself with a Caribbean cruise just because it sounds romantic. Pick suitable locations, not those that seem most impressive.

Finally, consider cost. Review your budget and determine what trips will provide the most satisfaction and keep you within your spending plan at the same time. Check out specials and discounted plans offered by travel agencies; just be careful with these, as many require you to make a long-term commitment to realize the discount. If a certain journey will take you over budget, can you make corresponding cuts in other areas to stay on track? You want your retirement to be healthy, long, and affordable. Staying on budget with travel will help you achieve your primary retirement goals.

66.

You and Your Domicile

In retirement, you may find that your home no longer suits you. Perhaps you're an empty-nester with too much space for a suddenly smaller family. Or you may be less interested in the expense and upkeep of a big house, preferring to allocate your physical and financial resources to more fulfilling retirement activities.

Still others continue to feel most comfortable in the dwellings that they've occupied for years, no matter how much excess space they may have. The good news about retirement is that you're free to choose the home that best serves you. You're no longer tied to a job or even a particular region.

There's much to consider about your living space. If your mortgage is paid off, you have the biggest home-related expense behind you, although you're still responsible for taxes and maintenance. You also have an asset that you can deploy for borrowing power. Should you decide to buy a new, perhaps smaller home, you may have to travel the mortgage route all over again. Apartment living brings a similar financial responsibility—monthly rent. While the sale of your home could help offset your new living costs, you'll want to carefully work through the finances before undertaking this new responsibility.

Think also about your comfort level. If you've lived in your current home for awhile, it may be a rich source of memories and satisfaction for you. You may value these above all—even if it means continuing to shovel snow from your long driveway in winter and mow your large lawn in the summer. Why abandon your memories for the sake of a more fashionable address? If your home is where your heart is, stay put.

Current house? New house? Apartment? Retirement community? You have a number of choices before you. All of them can be attractive and satisfying, and the great thing is that you can thoroughly review all of the options and make your decision at your leisure. Retirement isn't about avoiding important decisions, but it is about making choices in a relaxed atmosphere, free from pressure. That may be the best way to ensure that your house is always a home.

67.

Doing Something About the Weather

It's often said that you can't do anything about the weather—but where retirees are concerned, this venerable truism isn't necessarily true. You can do something about the weather. No, you don't have to soar skyward and seed the clouds or block out the sun, but you're in the enviable position of being able to pick the climate that's most congenial for you.

For most of your life, this may not have been the case. You may live where you do primarily for professional or family reasons. You might be tied to your community even if the climate is disastrous for you. Think of allergy sufferers forced to reside in locales with dense concentrations of allergens, or those in cold-weather cities who experience reduced mobility as temperatures plunge. These can be serious ramifications of weather.

Many retirees don't hesitate to change their personal weather; Florida and Arizona, with their year-round warmth, are prominent for their popularity with relocating retirees. Some try to combine the best of both worlds, living in their original homes during mild months, but shifting over to their retirement dwellings for the winter.

If you're considering relocating for reasons of weather, it's best to ponder the tradeoffs involved. The weather in your prospective new community may be more agreeable, but you'll pay a price—vast distances between you and your network of family and friends. While it's true that you'll form new friendships in any community that you adopt, it also may be true that they won't adequately replace those that you leave behind.

Think of weather as one element in your overall environment—a more comprehensive view that also includes social and family networks. When you adopt this broader perspective, you're more likely to select the locale that provides you with the most satisfaction.

68.

The Scoop on
Retirement Communities

If your home no longer suits you and you're pondering relocation, a retirement community may seem to be an attractive option—and it can be. You would be among people of roughly your own age and economic circumstances. You would have much in common with them, so that your new neighbors will probably become the social network that's so important to people in retirement.

However, because the number of retirement communities has grown so rapidly in recent years, finding the right place for you can require some research. Communities vary in many respects. Visit as many as you can, ask a lot of questions, and check out references.

In some retirement communities, for example, you'll purchase your own home and sell it when you choose, just as you would any other dwelling. Others may offer apartment or condominium living rather than for-sale homes. Still others may impose restrictions on the sale of your home, such as requiring approval by a homeowners' association. In extreme cases, the association may acquire the rights to your home after a certain number of years.

Scope of services and amenities is another area to probe. Some communities offer recreational lakes, libraries, vans to transport you wherever you'd like to go, convenience stores, restaurants, and even laundry and custodial services. They schedule trips to the local mall, nightly cookouts, and book discussions. This is a wonderful, community-oriented style—great, if that's what you're looking for. If you prefer a more private style with only occasional neighborly contact, make sure that your community accommodates that style.

While you're checking out style, look into prices for communal services. Some communities charge a monthly fee for such services as landscaping and snow shoveling. This may seem reasonable now, but is the price subject to change? If so, how are increases determined?

Finally, consider any "continuing care facilities." Some retirement communities are part of a larger organization that may include personal care, assisted living, and skilled nursing facilities—all located more or less on the same site. The concept is that if you need that type of care as you progress through retirement, it's all right there for you, allowing convenient transitions for you and your family.

Continuing care communities may even guarantee your admission to their other facilities when you purchase your retirement home. It's no fun pondering this issue, but if you make it part of your plans, it could spare you and your family from making a pressured, hurried choice should the need arise in the future.

69.

Explore Your Own Backyard

The notion of travel evokes picturesque images—majestic ships bobbing on placid blue seas, shopping bazaars bustling with bargains, fog-shrouded peaks off in the distance. All of this can be part of your travel plans—but so, too, can be the attractions in your own backyard.

This is referring, of course, to all of the wonderful things in and around your hometown. If your community is like most, it offers a wealth of riches that may include museums, historic battlefields, beautiful parks, off-the-beaten-path specialty shops, and wonderfully diverse restaurants. Chances are that while you were working, you were too busy to fully appreciate these attractions until an out-of-town visitor praised that charming little bistro a few blocks from your house, and you sheepishly replied that you had never been there.

It's very human to pine for distant attractions while ignoring those close to you. Now that you're retired, you have an excellent opportunity to become an expert on your own community.

If this type of local travel appeals to you, begin by making a list of interesting sites within a half-day's drive. The idea is not necessarily to visit all of the attractions on the list, but rather to give you a sense of their geography so that you can group several visits into a one-day excursion. Take a look through travel guides for your region to get a sense of the best travel routes, the hours of operation, and any costs involved.

Now you're set to explore. Day trips such as these offer several advantages. First, you can experience new things and be back in your own home by the day's end, if that's your pleasure. In addition, most day trips are affordable. They'll keep you within your budget while contributing to the sense of adventure that you expect from travel.

Perhaps best of all, you'll gain a deeper appreciation of your own community, the people who helped settle and develop it, and how visitors perceive your town. You'll become a one-person chamber of commerce, able to direct others to local sites that they're sure to find educational and entertaining.

70.

Perks Without Guilt

You probably know retirees who refuse to take advantage of the "perks" that society offers to them. When staying at a hotel, they don't flash their AARP cards to claim the discount. In fact, they may even disdain AARP membership. They don't call the community access van for reduced-price transport, and they wouldn't be caught dead at Early Bird dinner specials.

Pride may be at work here. Some people mistakenly equate acceptance of retiree perks with acknowledgment of a second-class, dependent status. Or perhaps they haven't yet come to grips with the changes in their lives. If they decline the benefits that society offers, they can maintain their images of themselves as valuable, hearty, contributing citizens.

While there may be a touch of nobility to this approach, it's fundamentally misguided. You are a valuable, hearty, contributing citizen; neither your retirement nor your acceptance of the benefits of your status changes that.

Think about all of the categories of people who receive special perks. Parents receive child-rearing breaks on their income taxes. The indigent receive public assistance that helps them buy groceries and pay the rent. Homeowners get breaks for any mortgage interest that they pay. Nor are society's advantages restricted to the underprivileged. Philanthropists earn tax breaks for their contributions to charity. Corporations may receive varied packages of tax breaks for locating in certain towns or states. The list of beneficiaries is just about endless.

Most perks are purposeful. Tax advantages are extended to corporations, for example, because it is recognized that the jobs which they create will have a positive impact that will far outweigh the money lost in the tax breaks given to them. Retiree perks have a purpose, as well—to make it as easy and convenient as possible for you to stay active and positive.

If this coincides with your objectives, why frustrate your own goals out of a misplaced sense of pride? Accept your perks without guilt. You've earned them.

71.

Pay Attention to Your Mail

When you retire, you face the danger of diminished regular social contacts. You no longer see your "work friends" on a daily basis, so you must build new social networks.

Just the reverse happens with postal contacts. Once you retire, you become the most popular target in town for mail. Every retirement community wants to tell you about its beautiful homes and amenities. Every trip organizer wants to sell you on the excitement of its travel packages. Every insurer wants to make you personally aware of the benefits of long-term care. Everybody, it seems, becomes your friend—through the mail.

Inevitably, there's a tendency to toss out every piece of direct mail, knowing that most will be a waste of time. However, if you do this, you may be throwing out the baby with the bath water. Useful information can come in the mail, so it's worth your time to sort through it carefully.

For example, it's not uncommon for municipal governments to introduce tax breaks for older residents. These may come in the form of property tax rebates, exemptions from local income tax, or relief from certain taxes and fees related to the sale of your home. Or perhaps your local government will decide to introduce a personalized transportation system for senior citizens. Typically, you'll be informed of that in a letter. If you pitch all of your direct mail without reading it, you may never learn of these opportunities. If you only rely on word of mouth, you may get information that's wildly inaccurate.

Another important piece of mail comes to you each year from the Social Security Administration, which provides a report on the taxes that you've paid and the benefits for which you qualify. Ignore your mail, and you'll miss this document, which can be vital to your financial planning.

Of course, now that you're retired, you'll be able to pay much more attention to news media; you'll pick up the thrust of any applicable tax breaks or programs from newspaper, TV, or radio reports. But you'll still need to know the details, and these typically will come to you in the mail.

Think of your mail as a potentially rich vein of precious metal. You'll need to invest some time in prospecting, but if you do, you'll unearth a few nuggets that will make it all worthwhile.

72.

Computers and Internet Options

When you take the plunge into the online world, you'll have plenty of options regarding equipment, software programs, and access to the Internet. It's easy to be overwhelmed by all of the choices, but you won't be confused if you treat your technology purchases just as you handle other major acquisitions. Gather all of the information that you need, get advice from experienced computer users—your kids and grandkids will be a valuable asset here—and pay attention to prices so that you can stick to your budget. As you conduct your research, here are some key points to consider.

Hardware—Think of your computer as a system: a processor, keyboard, monitor, printer, and modem that give you access to the Internet and other features. Prices and capabilities vary across a wide range. A good idea is to buy only as much computing power as you currently need. Sales representatives will try to sell you on the virtues of larger capacity so that your current system will suit you as your needs evolve. While this may be true, it's also true that each generation of computers soon becomes outdated. You'll be ready for a new system in a few years, whether or not your needs change. Refurbished computers and peripherals can be attractive options for beginners. You can learn on a retooled unit and save on the price.

Software—Software applications allow you to engage in word processing, implement tax programs, conduct desktop publishing—there's no end to their functionality. Remember that all software programs are proprietary, creative property developed by others. To use software programs, you must license them for a fee. Licensing the most popular software is relatively inexpensive but always required.

Internet access—You'll gain access to the Internet and the World Wide Web from an Internet service provider (ISP), which, for a monthly fee, will sell you "connectivity"—a connection to the Internet backbone that will link you with all other Net users. The most common and inexpensive type of connectivity is "dialup"—your computer will be outfitted with a modem that uses phone lines to dial up and connect to the Internet.

Other connectivity options include a digital subscriber line (DSL), which is offered by many phone companies and their resellers, and a cable modem, which is a feature of some cable television companies. DSL and cable access are faster than dialup service, but they're more expensive as a result.

All these new terms may be a bit confusing, but don't worry. Your tech team will help you through the jargon, and you will have more than enough choices to get you where you want to go.

73.

Your New Purchasing Power

It wasn't too long ago that product manufacturers—and the folks who developed their ads and measured consumer habits for them—routinely wrote us off when we reached the age of fifty. It was as if when you reached the telltale age of fifty, you fell from Consumers' Cliff, never again to be seen or measured by product makers. Even today, some radio and television stations focus on the under-fifty audience in promoting their space to potential advertisers.

Things have changed, however, and they are likely to undergo even more dramatic transformation. Today, there are 76 million Americans aged fifty and over. By the year 2030, it's projected that twenty percent of Americans will be sixty-five or older. It's quite clear that retirees represent a powerful and growing force in the consumer market—a force no longer to be ignored.

You can see the impact of this force in a number of ways. One of the more regrettable results, of course, has been the growing number of telemarketers and direct mailers targeting you and your fellow retirees. You will see it also in less intrusive forms of marketing and advertising. Today, the makers of products aimed at seniors routinely advertise during prime-time programs and other high-profile vehicles—expenditures that would have been considered wasteful only a few years ago. They host seminars for seniors, mount displays at shopping malls—in short, they're as intent on attracting seniors as they are in reaching out to other demographics.

This new emphasis on retirees helps you in several ways. First, it means that more product manufacturers are competing for your business. This competition results in the availability of a greater variety of goods and services—at better prices. Perhaps even more significantly, it means that you and your fellow retirees will be treated with respect in the marketplace. When you make a purchase or express satisfaction or displeasure with a product, you're not just voicing a personal opinion. You may well be speaking for 76 million people—most of them active, discriminating consumers. Now that's purchasing power!

74.

Work and Maintain
Social Security Benefits

For many years, retirees who continued to work part-time saw corresponding deductions in their Social Security benefits. This was a powerful disincentive for part-time work. If you had to, in effect, give back to the government a hefty percentage of your earnings, what was the point? Now that senior citizens have become an important and growing force in the workplace, the government has relaxed the rules on benefits reductions; the degree of liberalization depends on your benefits status.

If you're at full retirement age—currently sixty-five but rising to sixty-seven, depending on the year of your birth—you can earn as much as you want without losing any Social Security benefits. No ceilings, no limits, no fine print—you're still entitled to your full complement of Social Security benefits.

If you're not yet at full retirement but have begun receiving partial benefits, one dollar in benefits will be deducted for every two dollars that you earn above the annual limit. In the year 2002, the earnings limit was $11,280—a figure subject to yearly change.

In the actual year that you reach full retirement age itself, of course, you're home free—but if you report any calendar-year earnings for the months before you reach full retirement age, a dollar in benefits will be deducted for every three dollars that you earn above the limit for this category, which was $30,000 in 2002.

Here's an example. Let's say that you reach full retirement age in September 2002. Whatever you earned from January to August of that year is subject to the earnings test. If the total is less than $30,000, you're clear. If the total exceeds $30,000, the one-dollar-for three deductions kick in. When you visit the SSA web site, you'll find a calculator that will help you determine the impact of the earnings test on your Social Security benefits.

Keep in mind that in computing your earnings, you don't have to include pensions, dividends, interest, or distributions from IRAs or 401(k) plans. SSA defines income as "wages and earnings from self-employment."

Also remember that any money you earn in retirement is subject to Social Security taxes; you don't escape responsibility for these just because you're receiving Social Security benefits. However, because you're increasing your lifetime total for Social Security taxes paid, that may make you eligible for higher Social Security benefits—a neat little bonus for your determination and good work.

75.

A Budget Is More
Important Than Ever

Some people are able to sail through life without ever making a budget. They relegate excessive spending to credit cards—never mind that the bills and their killer interest charges come due eventually—or they have the wonderful knack of matching their spending with their income. For those of us who aren't quite that gifted, a budget provides both vital information and a reliable tool for developing spending discipline.

If budgeting is new to you, you'll find a series of useful budget templates in *The Newlyweds' Guide to Investing & Personal Finance* by Carrie Coghill Martin and Evan M. Pattak (Career Press, 2000). You may not be a newlywed, but these templates work in most situations.

You've evaluated your income, so you know how much money you have to work with. Now, take a stab at monthly expenses. Your allocation of costs may be vastly different than it used to be. Child-rearing expenses may be gone. Mortgage payments also may have vanished, although if you continue to own your own home, you'll never escape maintenance costs and taxes.

In place of such payments, you have new costs. For instance, you may never have included a "vacation" category before, instead spending whatever you needed for those annual trips. Now, if you hope to enjoy travel more regularly, you'll want to estimate the costs for your journeys. If you acquire a pet, you'll need to quantify associated costs—food and veterinary care chief among them. And if you've joined the Wired Nation, you'll need to add yet another new cost category—"office expenses." Printer paper, ink cartridges, Internet access, and computer maintenance may not seem like heavy hitters, but they can add up and should be accounted for. Finally, don't forget "savings" as a budget category; without savings, your money could run out before your retirement does.

Your budget will be your retirement spending plan. You'll know how much you can spend each month and where you would like to spend it—and you'll have the ability to make adjustments as needed. Budgets bring knowledge and control—both vital to a happy retirement.

76.
Be an Early Bird

Remember when you first glimpsed what your own retirement would be like? Your moment may have come at a restaurant. Arriving for an early dinner, you noticed that the place was packed with retirees there to enjoy Early Bird specials. Perhaps you vowed then that your retirement would be cushier than theirs; that you would never be forced to eat at 4:30 P.M. and pick your dinner from a reduced-portions menu.

Now that you've retired, you flash back to that vow you made and find that you're torn. Should you adhere to your pledge, or should you soften your approach and take advantage of Early Bird specials—and any other discounts offered to those of your status?

What's really at play here is image—how retirees are perceived, and how they perceive themselves. It is true that for years, retirees were an afterthought. Since retirements and lives were shorter than they are today, little thought was lavished on the needs of retirees—they wouldn't be around very long, would they? To much of society, retirees were largely invisible.

However unfortunate that perception was, it has been drastically updated. Retirees today are numerous and long-lived; many retirements will endure for as long as thirty years, making retirees a force to be reckoned with. They no longer live on the periphery of society's perception.

But what about your self-image? If you view early birding as a badge of shame, could it be that you need to work on that self-image? Could it be that you haven't come to grips with who you are in your retirement?

Retirement shouldn't change your self-image. You're a vital person, a valuable contributor to the social welfare with a range of talents and needs. Dig into that Early Bird special. Utilizing the discounts that are offered to you is enlightened consumerism—an indication of your savvy, rather than a badge of second-class status.

77.

Reining In Your Credit Cards

Credit-card debt is insidious. It appears to be nothing more than a harmless commitment to pay later for a purchase today, with a little interest charge tacked on. When you were younger and at the height of your earning power, debt may have been an acceptable price for immediate gratification. You could take on more work, generating more income to pay off debt down the road.

That may no longer be true of you in your retirement. You've walked away from your principal sources of income and might be hard-pressed to identify additional sources of cash. The impact of credit-card debt might be negligible today, but if it's unattended, it will lurk for awhile and then pounce, threatening your hard-earned retirement.

The figures on debt are persuasive. In the year 2000, the average debt in homes where the householder was sixty-five or older was $8,000, up 188 percent over the 1992 average, according to SRI Consulting Business Intelligence. While those figures include all debt—not just credit-card balances—the numbers are alarming.

When people retire, they typically do so with a wallet full of credit cards and monthly statements that may be bulging with interest charges. It's time to address both. Pay off your credit-card debt to the fullest extent possible so that you can begin your retirement with a clean slate. Without those spiraling interest charges, you'll be better prepared to stick to your budget—and you won't have debt hanging like a cloud over your retirement.

Also, give serious consideration to destroying most of your credit cards. This is not to suggest that you'll be able to avoid debt altogether. You may find that your retirement brings relocation and the need to finance a new home. Certainly, if you plan to engage in extensive travel, you'll need to purchase vehicles periodically and maintain them properly. This, too, may require you to take on some debt.

Can you draw the line there? Can you cut up most of your credit cards and commit to purchases on a cash-available basis? If you can, you'll be taking a major step toward a financially secure retirement.

78.

Retirement and Your Taxes

Wouldn't it be wonderful if on your last day of work, a representative of the Internal Revenue Service pumped your hand, congratulated you, and told you to forget about taxes for the rest of your life in honor of your distinguished career? The IRS is a friendlier group these days, but not *that* friendly. Your tax responsibilities will continue in retirement.

Paying tax bills always is a worry; that concern may deepen in retirement, when you may have less cash available to meet your obligations. In that situation, the tax tale becomes a good news/bad news story.

The good news is that with your salary gone, you're earning much less taxable income. As a result, you'll probably drop to a lower tax bracket, meaning that you're responsible for a smaller percentage of your income for federal income taxes. If you sell your home, you can realize up to $250,000 in capital gains ($500,000 for married couples) without triggering the capital-gains tax, provided that you've lived in that home for at least five years. At the state and local levels, you may be eligible for tax rebates, breaks on property taxes, and other benefits. One good reason for paying attention to your mail is to make sure that you receive and review news of local and state tax breaks for your age group.

On the downside, you may have new categories of income that could be subject to taxes. Social Security benefits fall into this category, as do distributions from certain types of IRAs. Remember all that you invested, on a tax-deferred basis, in that great 401(k) plan at work? Once you begin taking distributions, those taxes are deferred no longer.

Perhaps the best approach to taxes is to project what your obligation will be each year, and then make that estimate part of your budget. You even can adjust your income distributions from any IRAs or 401(k) accounts to ensure that you can accommodate the corresponding taxes. Death and taxes still may be life's certainties, but with careful planning, your taxes need not be deadly.

79.

How Much Should
You Withdraw?

For many, proceeds from investments can be a primary source of income in retirement. How much of those proceeds should you withdraw? Should you draw down the principal, as well? These are important questions for you as the manager of your retirement finances.

Some financial instruments require withdrawals when you reach a certain age. With traditional IRAs and nondeductible IRAs, for example, you must begin taking distributions at age seventy and a half. Roth IRAs, on the other hand, never require withdrawals; you can leave your account untouched and growing forever, if that's your choice.

Beyond mandatory withdrawals, your decision on distributions will be determined in large measure by your income needs. Let's suppose that your asset base is $500,000—a realistic number for many retirees today. If you can realize an average annual gain of five percent through effective management, your assets will produce $25,000 in income. Some retirees will find that an adequate sum to live on. They can withdraw the proceeds, leave the principal untouched, and achieve all of their retirement goals. (Remember that your distributions in many cases are taxable, so taxes must be factored into the mix.)

Others may find that $25,000 isn't sufficient for their needs, so they must tap part of the principal. This can work for now, but if your principal shrinks, it will be able to produce less and less income for the future. Thus, substantial withdrawals often bring a tradeoff—comfort now paid for by a less certain future.

It's also worth noting that while five percent annual growth may be a typical average performance, the operative word here is "average." You may experience years of smaller growth, years of no growth, or even years of losses. In lean years, you may be forced to reach into principal, even if that's contrary to your overall management policy.

Remember Murphy's Law of Retirement Finances: Money that can be spent *will* be spent. A good rule of thumb is to withdraw only what you need so that your principal remains as large as possible. If you keep it healthy, your asset base can be your financial workhorse throughout your retirement.

80.

Some Valuable
Travel Reminders

If you forget your toothbrush while packing, it probably won't mar your journey. You can purchase a toothbrush almost anywhere that you travel, so the omission is no big deal. However, there are several travel-related lapses—at either end of a journey abroad—that can transform your exciting voyage of discovery into a nightmare.

For example, don't forget to deal with visas while planning a trip abroad. Visas are the endorsements issued by your destination country indicating that your passport is in order and clearing your visit.

Many countries require visas—that means advance planning for you. You can acquire visa applications from any embassy, although engaging a visa service usually makes more sense. The key to success here is to apply in plenty of time. Visa approval must be stamped on your passport, so it's impossible to apply for more than one visa at a time. If you're hoping to visit several countries that all require visas, you must get started on your applications months in advance, or you could well be grounded.

At the back end of your trip, think about duties, the fees that you must pay on goods purchased abroad. If you're out of the U.S. for at least two days, you can bring back up to $400 worth of merchandise, duty-free. While you're away, you can mail back as many gifts as you want to family members, duty-free, as long as the contents of any package aren't worth more than fifty dollars.

Other than these exceptions, you'll be charged duty—the fee averages about ten percent of each item's purchase price, and it's due on the spot. If you don't have a receipt, customs inspectors will assign a value. If you're caught trying to cheat—submitting a phony receipt that deflates the value of an item, for example—the fine is six times the item's value. That's no way to end a rewarding journey, so be prepared to do your duty!

81.

Imposing Discipline

Retirement means freedom: freedom from waking up at a time determined by your employer, freedom from fighting traffic each day, freedom from a job that's less than fulfilling, freedom to be the person that you want to be. This liberation can be a wonderful thing, but it also can present a challenge. Just what are you supposed to do with all of this free time?

For some retirees, using their time will be a snap. They'll fill their days so full of productive activities that retirement will be an adventure of enrichment and self-realization. For others, however, the hours can hang heavy. This will be especially true of recent retirees who left staggering work schedules behind. Their career burdens afforded them little time to cultivate social relationships or hobbies; without their jobs, they don't know what to do with their lives.

If you ask successful retirees how they cope with this problem, many will answer with a single word: discipline. Of course, discipline is important in spending habits. To stick to your retirement budget, you need to curb your credit-card spending, cut costs wherever you can, and still put a little away for the future.

The tougher aspect of discipline may be imposing a schedule on yourself, and then sticking to it. While this may seem contrary to your initial notions about retirement, you soon may learn that approaching your days without a plan can lead to drift or boredom, or the even more dangerous feelings of frustration and resentment.

Your schedule need not be onerous. If you've launched an exercise program, for example, you may not need to work out seven days a week. However, if you plan for four days of physical activity, make every effort to get to the gym on those four days. Take the same approach with seeing family and friends. It may not be necessary to visit them every day, but it is important to develop a regular schedule of contacts.

"Disciplined retirement" is not an oxymoron. Rather, it's a philosophy that recognizes the importance of goals and achievement throughout your life. Work on that discipline until it becomes habitual. With a dollop of discipline, each of your retirement days will be a delight.

82.

Managing Your Investments

While you were working, you may have been a passive player in your own finances. If you participated in an employer-sponsored stock or pension program, such as a 401(k) account, you may have been content to designate a portion of your paycheck each week to the plan without regularly monitoring the results. Your account was growing, so perhaps you felt no urgent need to become actively involved in its management. Your career concerns were for the moment, while your retirement nest egg was for much later.

Much later has become right now, and it's the time to take control of your financial affairs. The status of your investment portfolio is more critical than it used to be. As a worker, your salary was your principal source of income and attracted the lion's share of your concern. Now that you've retired and have no salary, investment income can play a vital role in a comfortable retirement.

Get a handle on all of your investments—including savings accounts, stocks and bonds, IRAs, 401(k) accounts, annuities, whole-life insurance policies—and create a file for each investment. Get a feel for any mandatory withdrawals associated with your accounts; since you'll have no option on these, they're a good starting point for your planning.

Next, gather all current and past tax documents related to your investments. You won't be interested as much in the taxes as you will be in the annual reports for each investment. They'll provide you with a performance record that will help you evaluate your holdings.

Check titling and beneficiary designations for each investment. Your circumstances may have changed since you opened the accounts, so corresponding changes in titling and beneficiary may be appropriate. This won't produce more income for you now, but it will help ensure that your assets are directed properly upon your death.

Now you're ready to decide if your assets are doing the best job for you. Are they appropriately diversified to minimize your risk? Are they providing you with the dividends that you're counting on for your income package?

Many retirees devote a part of each day to studying their investments and the financial environment; this becomes a passion that brings them considerable satisfaction, as well as income. If crunching the numbers isn't for you, consider engaging a financial advisor to help. Whether you do it yourself or with professional assistance, active investment management should be a retirement priority.

83.

Spread Your Wealth

Retirement is often a time for repositioning assets. For example, you may want to begin taking distributions from an IRA for a 401(k) plan; in some cases, you'll be required to do so at a certain age, like it or not. Or you may need to liquidate some stock holdings and reallocate the proceeds to assets that produce more income now. Or you may receive a lump-sum retirement benefit or sell your house in favor of a smaller dwelling or a new community.

All of these events can bring significant infusions of cash that you may wish to deposit, however temporarily, in a bank account. Generally, there's little risk associated with bank accounts, as the Federal Deposit Insurance Corporation (FDIC) insures up to $100,000 in any one bank or savings association.

If your account is larger, there's no protection from the FDIC for the increment above $100,000. This is worrisome, and the concern has been underscored by recent bank failures. AARP reports that between 1999 and 2002, fifteen banks folded, affecting

$114 million in depositors' funds that were uninsured because the account balances exceeded $100,000.

Noting that many of the victims were retirees who had accumulated substantial assets, only to see them vanish, in 2002, the FDIC compiled a special report on this phenomenon. As part of the report, the FDIC advises you to divide your assets among several FDIC-insured banks so that you don't have more than $100,000 at any single institution. (It won't help to spread your money over different accounts at one bank, since the insured limit is $100,000 per financial institution.)

This may seem to be an inconvenience, since it will mean dealing with several banks, rather than one. However, now that you're online, you can consider electronic banking as an alternative to schlepping to the various banks that you'll be patronizing. Even if spreading your wealth is a bit awkward, it's a whole lot better than the potential alternative—losing much of that wealth in a bank failure.

84.

Who Has Your Power of Attorney?

Designating someone to execute your power of attorney is advisable at any age. It becomes even more vital for you in retirement, for several reasons. First, you tend to have more assets than you held when you were younger; all of those assets can be frozen for an uncomfortably long period if you become incapacitated and unable to render decisions. Also, you must acknowledge that the possibility of such tragedies looms larger as you age.

If you do experience an incapacitating injury or disease and you haven't executed a power of attorney document, your assets may be tied up until an appropriate court designates someone to manage your financial affairs. This can be an enormous hardship on your spouse and other dependents, who may find that they lack enough money for routine living expenses until the court rules. The impact can vary across the range of jointly held assets. For example, your spouse may be able to sell jointly held stock, yet be unable to write a check from a joint account.

Assigning your power of attorney is a relatively simple matter. Select someone that you trust for the job—that's the most important part. You're not limited to lawyers; anyone that you designate can administer your power of attorney.

Additionally, you may want to consider an advanced medical directive, which is to your health what a power of attorney document is to your financial affairs. The directive designates someone to make decisions about your medical care in the event that you become incapacitated; it also can specify the care that you want or don't want. For example, if you wish to forego extraordinary lifesaving efforts in the event of illness or injury, you can specify that in your directive.

Completing these documents can spare your family financial ravages and the tough decisions that they may be ill-prepared to make in the wake of emotions surrounding illness. These legal actions will help you maintain control over several important aspects of your life. Your retirement will be more enjoyable for that.

85.

Determine Your Travel Style

One of the things to ponder about your travel plans is whether to fly solo (or as a couple, if you're married) or to journey with a group. This reflects your travel style. There isn't any right answer—there may be as many styles as there are travelers to adopt them—but understanding your preferences up front will help you plan the most rewarding trips.

Do you enjoy exploring new sights on your own? Fashioning your own schedule rather than following a group itinerary? Eating what you choose, when you choose to eat it? If this sounds like you, perhaps you're better off traveling alone. On the other hand, if being with others deepens your understanding of and appreciation for new discoveries, and you prefer following an itinerary created by someone with more local experience than you, then you may thrive in group excursions with well-defined schedules.

Solo travel maximizes your options, but it also can be more expensive. You may be required to pay double-occupancy rates, or at least substantially more than half the standard charge for double occupancy. Pairing up with a companion could bring significant savings that help you stick to your travel budget. Your cruise or tour operator may even be willing to match you with another single traveler of the same sex.

Approach your style deliberations with an open mind. Consider the case of one traveler who was sure that he would hate any kind of group tour. Against his will, his wife booked them for a Caribbean resort that featured gentle athletic contests among the guests. His competitive instincts aroused, he got into it, carried home the gold, and enjoyed one of his most memorable trips. If you bring that sort of flexibility to your style, you may surprise yourself with how much you enjoy all of the options—each in a different way.

86.

Thinking About the Unthinkable

Few people feel comfortable pondering their own demise, yet creating a will—if you haven't already done so—is a critical retirement task. Thinking about the unthinkable may make you uneasy, but the alternative is even scarier. If you die *intestate*—the legal term for passing on without a will—your affairs will be settled according to the laws of your state. Your assets will go where a court directs—and you won't be around to object. It's far preferable to craft a will, however unpleasant the chore seems.

If you've reviewed your assets as preparation for retirement budgeting, you're already off to a good start. You're familiar with your savings vehicles, and you know the worth of each. Now, it's time to determine how you'd like to direct those assets. Family members are your most likely beneficiaries, but you also may want to bequeath money to friends and favorite causes. All of this can be codified in your will.

As for the actual document, off-the-shelf forms are readily available. These, however, tend to be one-size-fits-all documents that may not be appropriate for your situation. Your attorney can help you customize a will. In addition to directing your assets, you'll need to name an executor—someone to administer the provisions of your will. Clearly, your executor should be someone that you trust, someone of experience and integrity.

Beyond a will, here's a timely question to ask about your estate: If you're the one who handles financial affairs for your family, is your spouse familiar with all of your assets and aware of who to contact to gain access to those assets? If the answer is no, it's a great idea to prepare a list of key financial contacts. The list should include names, phone numbers, and e-mail addresses for attorneys, accountants, insurance agents, and financial advisors, as well as the accounts that they're handling for you.

If you're the spouse who isn't handling the family financial affairs, it's the right time to request such a list. The alternative is to scramble for information at a time of maximum stress—the death of your spouse—when you might not be at your most rational.

Thinking about the unthinkable won't be the highlight of your retirement. However, it will contribute to financial continuity for your family and peace of mind for you.

87.

The Fine Points
of Estate Planning

When you prepare a will, you've taken the most important step for the orderly disposition of your assets after your death. You can go even further and develop a sophisticated estate plan that preserves as much of your wealth as possible for your heirs by minimizing the taxes that they'll owe.

While federal inheritance taxes are on the wane—they're scheduled to be phased out entirely by 2010—this remains a fluid area. Congress can revisit the estate tax area at any time, so there's no telling what the law might require when your estate goes to probate. Moreover, inheritance taxes aren't the only potential responsibilities faced by your heirs. Consider those tax-deferred vehicles that you've been funding over the years, such as 401(k) plans and IRAs. If you die before you begin making withdrawals, your heirs will realize the growth in those vehicles, but they'll also be responsible for years of taxes that had been deferred.

There are good reasons for huddling with a financial advisor now to explore estate planning strategies. There are many of these, including establishment of trusts that can ease the tax burden. Gifting is another option. Under federal law, you can give up to $10,000 per year to each beneficiary that you choose without triggering any tax bill. Gifting is a perfectly legal way of diluting part of your estate now while reducing the tax obligation later.

When you were working, you may have been too busy and preoccupied to pay much attention to estate planning. You have the time and the motivation to do it now. Remember, estate planning isn't primarily for your benefit; it's for the continued well-being of your loved ones. That knowledge should be enough to inspire you to action.

88.

Dealing with Loss

In his timeless poem "The Love Song of J. Alfred Prufrock," T. S. Eliot pictured death as "the eternal Footman," ever ready to accept our coats and hats. It's a highly effective portrayal, wherein Eliot views the inevitability of death with wry humor. You'll have occasion to ponder the eternal footman in your retirement, which may be marked by the deaths of good friends.

The passing of friends is always difficult. Not only will you miss their company, but their deaths can be a sharp reminder of your own mortality. Rare is the person who reaches healthy maturity without experiencing this type of loss, but as you grow older, it will become a more frequent fact of life. You must confront this grim reality without letting it cast a pall on your retirement.

There are several ways to deal with loss that may help soften the impact. First, remember that you're not being singled out. Actuarial tables will show you that losses occur over time in any randomly selected group, and even among groups that aren't randomly chosen.

Networks based on residential proximity or a common employer, for example, all suffer losses over time. You're not alone in your grief. Loss of friends is a common experience; realizing that may help ease your burden.

Another way to cope with the death of a dear one is to celebrate your friend's achievements with others in your circle. You can capture their essence by gathering with other friends to remember and celebrate the lives of those departed. That will help you remember the good times and the joys that your friendships brought you.

Finally, you can transform your loss into action. Did your friend have a favorite cause or organization? You can perpetuate your friend's memory by donating—in money or time—to that entity. Did your friend leave family behind? You can extend your friendship by checking in with the family and offering to help out where you can.

You must understand that in your retirement, you're very likely to experience profound loss. If you develop the right outlook now, you'll be better prepared to cope with loss when it happens. Grief may strike you, but it won't paralyze you.

89.

Prioritize Your Health

See if this sounds familiar: You get home from work, play back your phone messages, and hear the cheery voice of your dentist's office manager reminding you that it's time for your six-month checkup. You hang up the phone with mixed feelings of irritation and guilt—irritation because you dread the thought of a session in the torturer's chair, and guilt because you know that you won't make that appointment. And you never do. You aren't feeling any discomfort, so why put yourself through the "drill drill"?

This may be characteristic of the way that you thought when you were young, but it's an attitude that you must update in your retirement. If you want your retirement to be as long and rewarding as possible, it follows that nothing is more important than your health. Put health concerns at the top of your retirement checklist.

In addressing your health, your top priority is to ensure that your medical insurance is appropriate for your situation. Review all of your insurance documents to familiarize yourself with your coverage. If you find any holes, now is the time to fill them.

Review your roster of doctors, dentists, and other professionals who may be treating you. Are these the professionals that you want to continue treating you during your retirement? Distance can be a concern here. When you were working, it may have been no problem to see an ophthalmologist across town because your work took you there frequently. In retirement, however, you may find that trip inconvenient and a deterrent to regular examinations. If that's the case, perhaps your doctor can recommend someone closer to your home.

Regular visits to your doctors should also be part of your emphasis on health. Mark all appointments on your calendar so that you'll have a record of them. That should help keep the time for your next appointment from slipping by unnoticed. You shouldn't be getting any more reminder notices from your doctors' offices; you'll be calling them before they even think of nudging you, because you'll be on top of your health.

90.

Don't Let Travel
Become Your New Boss

Travel can be intoxicating—and it can be exhausting, as well. The thrill of planning your journeys and then actually visiting new locales and exploring all of the sites can be heady. However, when you descend from the heights, you may find yourself weary, particularly if your journey involves significant time-zone changes that disrupt your body's habitual sleeping cycle.

If you find yourself dreading the next trip on your schedule, yet feeling compelled to take it because you don't want to lose any deposits or consider yourself a disappointment for pooping out, it may be time for adjustments. This is not an indication of failure in any way. Rather, it's a rational response to your changing needs.

Travel fatigue doesn't mean that you must forego exploring entirely. You can, for example, cut back on the frequency of your excursions to give yourself ample time to recover. Or you can emphasize day trips rather than lengthy journeys for awhile. With shorter journeys, you'll experience the joys of travel while reducing the physical and mental stress that extended travel can bring.

Another approach is to take all of the trips that you planned but make them a little less demanding. Some travelers overschedule themselves, wanting to drink in everything there is to experience by cramming it into a few hectic days. Their thinking is that they may never get back to these exotic and wonderful lands, so they don't want to miss anything.

If this type of blitz works for you, that's great, but if you find that overscheduling diminishes your fulfillment and adds a stress factor, kick back. Take a more relaxed approach. Plan a comfortable activities schedule that leaves plenty of time for lazing and lingering over meals. Travel is not a test; you don't flunk if you don't visit every cathedral, museum, or fort.

You want to enjoy travel, not be ruled by it. If travel becomes your new boss, you haven't really retired.

91.

Exercise but Don't Overdo It

Y ou've always known that physical fitness is in your best interest, but the pressures of the job made it almost impossible to commit to a daily exercise schedule. If you could carve out a few hours for exercise, you found yourself too tired to do much of anything.

All of that's behind you now; you're well-positioned to plan and implement a regular schedule of physical activity. If you're tempted to dive right in and make up for all of those sedentary years in one frantic burst of effort, slow down. Fitness is a lifelong process, not a one-day wrecking crew. You'll do yourself more harm than good by taking on too much too soon.

Begin moderately—just a few minutes will do for starters. You can add to your workout each day, so long as you keep feeling good. Remember your goals here. You're not targeting the Olympic trials, so you should pay no heed to the notion of "no pain, no gain." This may be true for world-class athletes striving to build muscle, but you won't require pain to achieve your goals—a strong heart and circulatory system, comfortable body weight, and a general feeling of well-being.

Which activities should you choose? For some, exercise in retirement will be an extension of activities, such as golf, already enjoyed for many years. If you're just beginning to exercise, think of walking—a great way to prepare for just about any other exercise—or birding, which can combine exercise and nature study. For the challenge and novelty of it, try an exercise that has always seemed completely outrageous to you—fencing, for example. You'll round out your talents and experience, even as you become fit.

Consider which exercise venues work best for you. Some people prefer to purchase home exercise equipment and work out in private. Others enjoy the amenities of public fitness centers, which typically offer a variety of classes in such activities as aerobics, water aerobics, and dance. Group exercise will keep you fit—and extend your network of new friends.

92.

Focus on Wellness

Throughout your busy career, you may have paid scant attention to your physical well-being. You prioritized family and work concerns to such an extent that your own health was relegated to minor-league status. When you attended to your health at all, it was on an "as-needed" basis—if you got sick, you sought out a quick fix so that you wouldn't miss too much work.

This is a case of misplaced priorities. After all, if ill health overtakes you, you can't be very effective on the job or with your family. Fulfillment on those fronts begins with your continued good health.

Your retirement brings you an excellent opportunity to realign your priorities and focus on your health—not on treatment alone, but on the broader concept of "wellness" and its emphasis on prevention. Wellness involves several key components that produce sound functioning of mind and body and the confident attitude that's a product of excellent health.

Exercise is one component—the kind that improves your circulation, heart rate, and self-confidence, not the kind that leaves you with perpetual muscle aches and discomfort. Nutrition is another vital element. If meals have been rushed affairs for you, or if you ate what was convenient rather than what was best for you, you now have the time for a different approach. Plan your meals. Dedicate some time to thorough grocery shopping so that you have all of the necessary raw materials for nutritious eating. As you do with all other aspects of retirement, bring creativity to your shopping and eating habits. This will provide you with the satisfaction of tasks well-planned and achieved—as well as a more balanced diet.

Don't ignore sleep as part of your wellness program. If you felt the effects of chronic sleep deprivation throughout your career, now's the perfect time to improve your sleep habits. Experiment a little. Figure out your optimum hours of sleep each night, and then determine to get just that much sleep—neither more nor less.

When you get into your wellness routine, you may even find that certain activities may be covered by your health insurance. Expenses for fitness club membership ordinarily would not be covered, but if your physician prescribes a therapeutic massage program, those costs could be reimbursable. Should your study of your sleep habits reveal a breathing malfunction, that treatment, as well, may be covered. If you find that you can recover some of your out-of-pocket wellness expenses, then you will really feel good.

93.

Your New Approach
to Health Insurance

Many retirees find themselves in a no-man's-land of health care where they're too young for Medicare but no longer working and protected through employer plans. If your spouse continues to work, and you're covered through your partner's plan, your needs are provided for. However, if you're both retiring simultaneously, or if you're a single retiree, health insurance should command your attention as soon as possible.

Clearly, you'll need to consider health-insurance options well before you retire so that enrollment in your new plan will coincide with your retirement. As you explore those options, you may find that your coverage costs could increase dramatically. You may also find that the individual plans offered to you are less comprehensive than those that your employer provided. Vision and dental care, for example, may not be part of the general coverage offered.

The one piece of good news about private plan enrollment is that you won't face discontinuation of reimbursements for "preexisting conditions." This potential gap in coverage has largely been closed by recent legislation.

Some retirees will be eligible for ongoing coverage through their employers under COBRA, the Consolidated Omnibus Budget Reconciliation Act of 1986. If you qualify, you may receive up to eighteen months of COBRA coverage, although your former employer won't be contributing at all. In fact, the company can collect up to 102 percent of the costs from you to recoup their administrative expenses.

Often, a better option is to join a large group that offers health-insurance plans. AARP has such a program, as do many business trade groups. Insurers welcome sizable voluntary organizations. Because they're getting so much business from these groups, insurers are able to offer more comprehensive coverage—and at better rates—than you might find as an individual.

Now that you're online, you can visit the web sites of these organizations and review the health plans that they offer. Take the time to compare plans. Do they offer vision and dental care? Is the full range of mental-health services covered? What are their policies on preexisting conditions? Is their coverage HMO-based, and if so, are your physicians in the network? Explore these questions and more. Of course, you'll want to compare rates, as well, but where your health is concerned, money may not be the principal driver in your selection of a new insurance plan.

94.

Take Advantage of Drug Discounts

As the number of retirees has grown, so, too, have the benefits available to them. Alas, access to affordable prescription drugs isn't necessarily among those benefits. According to AARP, prescription drug spending is soaring at about seventeen percent per year—the biggest culprit in health-care inflation.

There are many reasons for this, including development of new drugs that are more expensive than those they replace and the election of drugs rather than surgery as treatment protocols for certain ailments. Some observers also blame massive advertising by drug makers—calculated by AARP at nearly $2.5 billion in the year 2000 alone—that leads consumers to name-brand drugs rather than their less expensive generic counterparts.

Perhaps most significantly of all, access to affordable prescription drugs is not yet a benefit of Medicare, despite a number of high-level attempts to make it so. There will no doubt be further legislative movement on this front, but the fate of any such initiative is unclear.

There is some good news here. In 2002, seven leading pharmaceutical companies introduced a drug discount program called "Together Rx." The program is open to Medicare participants without drug coverage and offers discounts on more than 150 products, with each participating company determining its own discount schedule. The program does have income limitations, and it restricts discounts to the products of participating companies. For more information on Together Rx, you can call (800) 865-7211 or visit the web site (www.togetherx.com).

Apart from this program, two other drug makers, Pfizer and Eli Lilly, offer flat-fee co-payment cards on prescriptions for their own products.

These discount programs are worth exploring, as are generic equivalents for the medications that you may need. When your physician prescribes a drug, it's useful to discuss the possibility of a generic version. You might realize significant savings—particularly if the medication is part of a long-term treatment plan.

95.

A Beautiful Day
in the Neighborhood

Sometimes, you can extend your social network simply by knocking on your neighbors' doors. That's because many people don't know their neighbors very well. Just as you've been working hard to finance and prepare for your retirement, some of your neighbors probably have been occupied with similar pursuits. You may have been like the proverbial ships passing in the night: a quick hello at the driveway; a wave as you take out the trash; a card at the holidays. In fact, the very notion of the American neighborhood—that warm, special place that protects and nurtures—isn't nearly as compelling as it was to previous generations.

You have a wonderful opportunity now to restore that unique sense of place. Spend time with your neighbors. Instead of nodding at them and going about your business, make socializing with them your business. Walk across the yard for a nice, leisurely chat. Invite them to your home to do the same. Think about barbecues, block parties, and other community-building events. With your organizational skills, you can become the key planner for such events, performing a valuable service for your friends.

Don't limit your definition of "neighbors" to those in adjacent homes. If you think of "neighborhood" in a broad sense, you'll find that it includes people you may have taken for granted when your career was your top priority. Consider your postal and newspaper carriers. Do you know their names, their backgrounds, the aspirations of these folks who have served you so long? Retirement is a great time to reach out to them as you broaden your social circle.

Don't despair if it takes you a while to get the hang of all of this neighborliness. It may represent a fundamental shift in attitude and behavior for you—a transformation that you won't accomplish overnight. However, affection and concern for your neighbors will soon come more naturally. Before long, you'll find that every day is a beautiful day in your neighborhood.

96.

Is Long-Term Care
Insurance for You?

There are more retirees than ever before, and they're living longer than their ancestors did. That's great news—they're staying healthier deep into old age. Yet this also means that more people may require long-term care at the end of their lives, and at significant expense.

The price of long-term care can be staggering. If you and your spouse require it simultaneously, costs can range as high as $50,000 per year or more, depending on the type of care required or selected. This can be a major blow to you, as well as your family, if they're helping you choose and finance your long-term care.

The insurance industry has developed a product for such situations —long-term care insurance. Having such coverage can bring tremendous peace of mind. You'll know that the needs of you and your spouse will be met without bankrupting your family. But is this type of coverage for you? It's worth it to begin exploring policies now.

Price will be one factor to look at. Premiums may be less expensive than you imagine. A couple in their forties, for example, can acquire coverage for about $100 a month, in some cases. At $1,200 a year, you can pay premiums for the next twenty-five years and still spend less than you might on a single year of long-term care for you and your spouse. How can insurers offer such attractive rates? Their research tells them that long-term care is something of a misnomer. Long-term care typically doesn't last that long, so they're doling out the benefits for short periods relative to the many years that they have to collect premiums.

Some policies cap benefits, and they may limit the types of care that they'll cover. Skilled nursing care and assisted living, when recommended by a physician, typically are covered. Home care and personal-care facilities may not be, especially where they haven't been specifically prescribed by your doctor.

As with all insurance policies, you'll want to weigh the costs and benefits. Call insurers to have your questions answered; you'll find them eager to meet with you at your convenience. Bring your family into the discussions. Your children will appreciate the opportunity to work with you on a plan for your care rather than be forced into an immediate decision should the need arise. You may also find that you'd like to consider long-term care plans for your own parents as well—an added benefit of your timely research.

97.

Keep a Travel Journal

One of the byproducts of frequent travel is that trips of the recent past tend to be displaced by current adventures. No matter how sharp your impressions, no matter how vivid the sights when you were there, these memories tend to recede as you encounter new wonders. This can be disconcerting, as your travel accomplishments tend to lose their luster if you can't recall them clearly.

A great remedy for this is a travel journal that records and preserves your experiences, impressions, and conclusions. Your journal doesn't have to be fancy, but it should be handy—a reporter's notebook, for example, that you can carry with you as you explore. Then when a thought strikes you, you can whip out your journal, record your insight, and return the journal to your pocket. It's an unobtrusive way of preserving your thoughts. A tape recorder is a workable alternative if you prefer speaking your thoughts to writing them. If upon your return home you want to flesh out your thoughts and record them in a more permanent format—such as a computer document, for instance—you'll have that opportunity.

Include your sensory observations, of course, but don't limit your journal to these. Note your thoughts on the people that you encounter, their lifestyles and customs, and how they perceive you. Record dialogue, as well—your tape recorder will help you there. That will add some flavor and spice to your journal.

You'll find that a journal deepens your appreciation for the lands that you've visited even as it provides a basis for comparison. As you explore a new country, you can use your journal to compare your current thoughts to your reactions to other countries. Recording also will make you a sharper observer. Knowing that you intend to take notes will keep you focused on the defining characteristics of each place that you visit.

Above all, your journal will contribute to your sense of achievement. Each time that you open it, your journal will affirm that travel is a rewarding learning experience for you, not a means of idling away time.

Think of yourself as the travel editor for your own newspaper. It's likely that this newspaper won't have any subscribers but you and those close to you, but if you maintain a travel journal, you'll be doing exactly what professional travel writers do. It isn't such a stretch to imagine sharing your observations with a broader audience.

98.

Take Stock of Your Retirement

As with any other period of life, retirement can require adjustments. During your career, you seldom had the time to ask the fundamental questions about your circumstances and whether they were contributing to your fulfillment. In retirement, you have plenty of time to take stock—and to plan and implement appropriate changes.

Budget is an obvious area for constant monitoring and tweaking. As your income and needs change, you must make the corresponding modifications in your retirement budget. Some prefer to do this annually; but by the time your once-a-year budget review rolls around, you may have spent yourself into a corner. Take a cue from corporations here and employ a quarterly "forward look" to track your spending and income versus budget. Your adjustments may be smaller and less painful if imposed every three months.

Just as important is an evaluation of the progress that you're making toward your retirement goals. For example, are you involved in as diverse a schedule of activities as you had hoped? If not, then it's time to consider taking on some new and exciting challenges.

Have you achieved a desirable balance between time for yourself and time spent socializing? This point won't require extensive analysis. If you find yourself feeling lonely and out of every loop, you'll know that it's time to pay more attention to family and friends and to seek out new relationships and networking opportunities.

How about travel? Have you found a happy medium—one that allows for frequent journeys but also saves sufficient time for family gatherings and community service? You can adjust your travel schedule quite easily, enhancing or trimming it as needed. (If you're cutting back, though, don't forget about any fares or fees that you may have paid in advance; nobody wants to lose those needlessly.)

The key thing to remember is that this new period in your life is not a constant state. Retirement is as dynamic as you are. Your goals—and your methods for achieving them—most likely will evolve. If you take periodic stock of your retirement, you'll be well-positioned to keep your goals and activities in sync.

99.

Your Own Oral History

You've seen much in your day, witnessed many changes, enjoyed some triumphs, and endured some tragedies. Your life would be a terrific topic for a book or movie, but the reality is that most people won't be the subject of formal biographies. So why not create your own life story through an oral history?

If you're tape recording your impressions when you travel, you've already mastered the only technological tool that you really need for an oral history, and your travel notes will provide a solid foundation for your informal life story. Now you can build on that by creating a record of the major developments of your life. Include important family, career, and retirement events, but get beyond the plot, as well. Talk about your friends, your impressions, your feelings, your satisfactions and regrets, and above all, the conclusions that you've drawn from your experiences. These are the sorts of insights that a biographer would seek.

In a sense, your oral history never will be finished because you continue to create your life story each day. However, at a certain point, you may want to formalize your history by transcribing the tapes—even editing them a bit to provide a more compelling narrative.

The process of remembering and analyzing your life will deepen your appreciation for friends and family, enhancing your own self-awareness en route. When you force yourself to conclusions about your life, you may unearth feelings that were unarticulated until now. You'll have a tangible record of your life that your children and their children will cherish—and from which they'll learn.

Oral histories are powerful. Imagine that all of your former colleagues joined you in compiling oral histories. Preserved in one book, they would provide a unique and insightful look at what it meant to live in your community, to work for your company, and to be alive at a particular time. That would be a valuable tool for historians and scholars—and a reminder to you and your friends that your lives have been noteworthy.

100.

The Challenges of Retirement

Retirement seems easy—but only to those who haven't been there yet. *You* know the challenges involved in fashioning and sustaining a happy and rewarding retirement—because that's just what you've created for yourself. Think of what you've accomplished.

Through careful planning and even some sacrifices, you saved a nest egg to help finance the retirement that you always envisioned. Even now, you're sticking to a sharp retirement budget and salting away even more funds for the future.

You've built your retirement on an upbeat, can-do attitude, taking responsibility for your own happiness. You've prevented the isolation that retirement can bring by staying in touch with friends and establishing fruitful new relationships. You're closer to your family than ever before, which provides a deeper level of contentment than you might have thought possible.

You're contributing your time and talent to civic, charitable, and neighborhood organizations, giving back to the community the support that it offered you throughout your career. You're a "Netizen," a dedicated and able user of the Internet, and you've mastered those technological tools that are most valuable to you.

You've broadened your knowledge and perspective through travel, hobbies, and the pursuit of many other interests that were pushed to the back burner during your career. You're becoming the person that you always wanted to be.

Your retirement has been remarkable—and you'll accomplish still more as this astonishing period of your life progresses. Take a bow. You've done well.